1 MONTH OF
FREE
READING

at
www.ForgottenBooks.com

By purchasing this book you are eligible for one month membership to ForgottenBooks.com, giving you unlimited access to our entire collection of over 1,000,000 titles via our web site and mobile apps.

To claim your free month visit:

www.forgottenbooks.com/free174959

ISBN 978-0-265-18051-8
PIBN 10174959

himself by Jesus Christ, and hath given to us the ministry of reconciliation; to wit, that God was in Christ, reconciling the world unto himself, not imputing their trespasses unto them; and hath committed unto us the word of reconciliation. Now then we are ambassadors for Christ, as though God did beseech you by us: we pray you in Christ's stead, be ye reconciled to God. For he hath made him to be sin for us, who knew no sin; that we might be made the righteousness of God in him."

This is an authentic description of the mission of Christ to the inner life of man. This is a reflection of what He really effected in the secret place of the human heart. This is the voice of that new tide of peace which silently rose through man's experience, — *The original gospel.*

> "One common wave of thought and joy
> Lifting mankind again."

This is the original gospel, which began to win the world eighteen hundred years ago, and has never ceased to spread from heart to heart, from land to land, like music mixed with light.

And it is the faithful and persistent witness to this experience, more than anything else, that has made Christianity a world-religion. A changed heart, uttering its new-found fe-

THE GOSPEL FOR
A WORLD OF SIN

WORLD OF SIN

A COMPANION-VOLUME TO
"THE GOSPEL FOR AN AGE OF DOUBT"

BY

HENRY VAN DYKE

D.D. (PRINCETON, HARVARD, YALE), LL.D. (UNION)
PASTOR OF THE BRICK CHURCH IN NEW YORK

New York
THE MACMILLAN COMPANY
LONDON: MACMILLAN & CO., Ltd.

1918

Norwood Press
J. S. Cushing & Co. — Berwick & Smith
Norwood Mass. U.S.A.

To

JAMES ORMSBEE MURRAY

DEAN OF PRINCETON UNIVERSITY

A TEACHER OF LITERATURE AND LIFE

A PREACHER OF RIGHTEOUSNESS AND LOVE

A SERVANT OF HUMANITY AND CHRIST

This Book is Dedicated

IN GRATEFUL AFFECTION

PREFACE

THIS book is not meant to present a theory of the Atonement.

On the contrary, it is meant to teach that there is no theory broad or deep enough to embrace or explain the fact.

A sinful world cannot possibly know all that is needed to reconcile it with a holy God.

Sin itself, in its root and in its relations, contains a mystery.

So does love.

But the Atonement is the work of God's love in its bearing upon man's sin. Therefore it must include more than we can explain.

What Christ did to take away the sin of the world was precisely all that was needed, — neither more nor less. What we know of this need is what we know about the Atonement.

One man sees one segment of the circle more clearly. Another man sees another segment.

No man sees the whole circle.   But if each one sees his little arc of experience in right relation to the centre, he sees it as part of the truth.

The false theories of the Atonement are those which claim to be final and exclusive. That claim breaks the line of curvature and conceals the true centre.

The saving work of Jesus Christ for man as a sinner, — that is what the Atonement means to us.   I think it surpasses all explanations of it, just as life is more than biology.

HENRY VAN DYKE.

THE BRICK CHURCH MANSE,
NEW YORK CITY,
February 28, 1899.

CONTENTS

I

THE MIST AND THE GULF

Tho' Sin too oft, when smitten by Thy rod,
Rail at 'Blind Fate' with many a vain 'Alas!'
From sin through sorrow into Thee we pass
By that same path our true forefathers trod;
And let not Reason fail me, nor the sod
Draw from my death Thy living flower and grass,
Before I learn that Love, which is, and was,
My Father, and my Brother, and my God.

—ALFRED TENNYSON, *Doubt and Prayer.*

I

THE MIST AND THE GULF

DOUBT is the blinding mist that rises between *Doubt and sin.*
man's spiritual vision and the eternal truth.

Sin is the great gulf that separates man's
moral character from the divine ideal.

The mists gather, and thicken, and melt, and
disperse. The gulf is always there. Ages of
doubt come and go, in an abiding world of sin.

The pain of doubt is an evidence that man
was made for faith. The shame of sin is an
evidence that man was created for holiness.

A gospel for humanity must be good news *A sympathetic gospel.*
both for doubters and for sinners. The depth
of its sympathy will always be the measure of
its power.

It must not condemn doubt as if it were a
sin : neither must it deny sin as if it were
merely an illusion of doubt.

To doubting men and to sinful men it must
speak the message of a divine love, — a revealing love that pierces the mist with rays of
light and brings clearness and joy to the con-

fused and darkened spirit, — a redeeming love
that bridges the gulf of separation and leads
the guilty conscience back into peace and harmony with God.

*Doubt is
transient.*
An age of doubt is a transient phase of a sinful world.   There is always some doubt in the
world, just as there is always some moisture in
the air.   At certain times and in certain places
this moisture is increased and rolls together in
gray mist and clinging fog.

There are certain stages and conditions of
human thought in which the difficulties of believing in a spiritual world are multiplied and
grow more dense and impenetrable.   The soul
of man seems to be shut in by a narrower horizon.   Things that are near loom larger in the
mist.   Things that are far are lost to view.
The atmosphere in which the spirit moves is
heavy and bewildering.   Men are confused,
hesitating, questioning, despondent, in regard
to all that lies beyond the reach of the senses.
Doubt, always present though diffused, becomes
so thick and pressing, that it overshadows the
age.

Through such an age I think we have been
passing, in this latter half of the nineteenth
century.   Of the intellectual causes which have

led to this increase of doubt ; of the qualities which characterize it, — qualities for the most part sympathetic and hopeful, — its reverence for the questioned faith, its deep unrest and sorrow, its loyalty to ethical ideals ; and of the gospel which it needs, the gospel of the personal Christ clearly revealing the reality and fatherhood of God, the liberty and responsibility of man, and the immortality of the soul, — of these things I have written in a former book.

But such a presentation of the gospel, from the point of view of a particular age, and with the purpose of meeting certain intellectual needs, certain urgent questionings of the human spirit, could not be (and indeed it was not intended to be) complete and sufficient. Man has other needs than those of the intellect. After the question of the reality of God is answered, then remains the question of our personal relation to Him.

The age of doubt will pass, is already passing, and we are entering, if the signs of the times fail not, upon a new era of faith. *The dissolving of doubt.*

There is a renaissance of religion. Spiritual instincts and cravings assert themselves and demand their rights. The loftier aspirations, the larger hopes of mankind, are leading the

new generation forward into the twentieth
century as men who advance to a noble conflict and a glorious triumph, under the cap-
taincy of the Christ that was and is to be.
The educated youth of to-day are turning with
a mighty, world-wide movement toward the
banner of a militant, expectant, imperial
Christianity. The discoveries of science, once
deemed hostile and threatening to religion, are
in process of swift transformation into the
materials of a new defence of the faith. The
achievements of commerce and social organization have made new and broad highways around
the world for the onward march of the believing host. Already we can discern the brightness of another great age of faith.

When doubt   But an age of faith, when the mist of doubt
dissolves,   is dissolved and driven away, is always the time
sin is made
clear.   when the gulf of sin is most clearly visible.

The souls that are most sure of the reality of
God and the future life are always those that
feel most deeply their separation from Him and
their guilty uncleanness in His sight. The evil
that is in their own hearts presses upon them
more heavily, the more vividly they realize the
actual existence of the spiritual realm and its
eternal significance. The evil that is in the
world does not disappear nor change, through

all the coming and going, the darkening and *Sin also* dissolving of human doubts in regard to its *needs a* origin, nature, and meaning. It remains an *gospel.* unalterable fact in human experience. The interpretation which religious faith gives to it intensifies the necessity of a divine salvation from it.

Those who have accepted the gospel for an age of doubt are those who feel most keenly the need of the gospel for a world of sin.

There cannot be two gospels. I do not believe *The unity of* that there is any essential difference or contra- *all gospel in* diction between the message which Christianity *Christ.* has for one age and that which it has for another. It is always the glad tidings of the personal Christ, the revealer of God and the Saviour of men. The application of this mes- sage is as wide and various as human need and longing, hope and fear, sorrow and sin.

To those who are doubtful and confused, to those who have lost the sense of spiritual things, the divine voice says, "This is my be- loved Son; hear him."[1]

To those who are sinful and sorrowful, upon whom the sense of evil rests like an intolera- ble burden, the voice says, "Behold the Lamb

[1] Luke ix. 35.

of God, which taketh away the sin of the
world." [1]

*Christ the
Revealer is
Christ the
Saviour.*

These two elements of the gospel are interwoven and inseparable.   Christ could not take
away the sin of the world unless He were the
Son of God.   Christ would not be the divine
Saviour unless He took away the sin of the
world.

In trying to set forth the personal Christ as
God's answer to the doubts and questionings
of this age, I could not help speaking of Him
as the deliverer from sin.[2]   Nor will it be possible to present His sacrifice on the cross as the
world's redemption without confessing a constant faith in Him as God manifest in the flesh.

*Companion
volumes.*

Indeed, this second book is written chiefly
because I feel the need of a fuller utterance
to complete the message of the former book.
I would have the two books stand together
and interpret each other.   They are but win-
dows looking toward Christ from two different points of view.

The message of the first book was this:
Christ saves us from doubt, because He is the
revelation of God.

The message of the second book is this:

---

[1] John i. 29.

[2] *The Gospel for an Age of Doubt*, pp. 75 ff., 162 ff.

Christ is the revelation of God, because He saves us from sin.

Many of the men and women whom the *The preacher's sympathy.* preacher meets to-day are or have been doubters. All are sinners. He must speak out of his own heart to theirs. His word must have the comfort which can only come from one who has been comforted, the peace which can only be declared by one who has sought and found it in the experience of reconciliation with God, the sympathetic power which can only flow from one who knows both the burden of iniquity and the blessedness of forgiveness through Christ.

The gospel for a world of sin cannot be preached by any except those who need it for themselves. An angel could not deliver it aright. Its language is always in the first person plural, drawing the speaker and the hearers into a brotherhood of penitence and forgiveness.

"God commendeth his love toward *us,* in that, while *we* were yet sinners, Christ died for *us.*"[1]

Christ Himself did not come to preach this gospel.

[1] Romans v. 8.

He came to live it.

It was when the Apostles Peter and Paul and John had seen Him delivered for their offences and raised again for their justification that they began to understand and preach this gospel for a world of sin. Ever since it has had but one message.

" *Through his name whosoever believeth in him shall receive remission of sins.*" [1]

"*God was in Christ reconciling the world unto himself.*" [2]

"*If any man sin, we have an advocate with the Father, Jesus Christ the righteous : and he is the propitiation for our sins, and not for ours only, but also for the sins of the whole world.*" [3]

---

[1] Acts x. 43.   [2] 2 Cor. ii. 19.   [3] 1 John ii. 1, 2.

II

THE SIN OF THE WORLD

Judge me not as I judge myself, O Lord!
  Show me some mercy, or I may not live:
Let the good in me go without reward;
  Forgive the evil I must not forgive.

       — WILLIAM DEAN HOWELLS, *Conscience.*

II

THE SIN OF THE WORLD

THE sins of the world are many. The sin of *The solidar-*
ity of sin.
the world is one.

It is like the grass of the field. Below the separate shoots and blades, which stand up individual and distinct, as if each one grew by itself, there is a network of branching roots and fibres, knotted together, interwoven, tenacious, spreading far, and propagating itself more swiftly the more it is cut and divided. The separation is on the surface. The unity is underground.

But before we can have any idea of what sin means, either separately in the individual or collectively in the race, we must give some thought to the problem of evil, starting not from the point of view of philosophy, but from the point of view of experience.

13

I

The Presence of Evil

The hidden root. Beneath all the particular forms of evil that exist in the world, men have always recognized a common ground of evil in human nature. Something has happened to the race, something has entered into it and taken possession of its vital powers, which makes it bring forth bad fruit. This is not a theory. It is a fact.

The experience of mankind, thus far, is a mass of cumulative evidence that there is a radical twist in humanity which runs through it from top to bottom, and produces crooked results in every sphere of human life. So far as we can judge by our own experience, and by observation of others, every child of man who comes to moral consciousness, comes not only with a freedom of will which makes the choice of evil possible, but also with a propensity which makes such a choice probable. This probability is so strong that we always reckon with it, in dealing with ourselves or with others.

No man gets fairly started in the journey of life without knowing that he has a tendency to go wrong. It is the folly of the fool that he

forgets it.   The wise man remembers, fears,
and tries to guard against it.

Human society is organized around two facts: *Society on
the desire of good and the recognition of evil. guard.*
Every institution in the world which is of any
value has in it a defensive, corrective, punitory
side, which is an unconscious confession that
mankind is prone to do wrong.   Men take this
for granted in all the relations of life.   Whether
they are making systems of education or of
government, whether they are devising enter-
prises to increase their property, or laws to
protect it, or wills to distribute it, they always
take into account the fact that there is a strain
of evil running through all humanity.

The advance of modern science and philos- *The warn-
ophy has not reduced or weakened the evidence ing of philosophy.*
of this common ground of evil in the world.
On the contrary, it has done much to deepen
and intensify the conviction that there is a radical twist in human nature.   The easy-going
and superficial optimism of the eighteenth century is thoroughly discredited and obsolete.
Men have turned away from Rousseau's skin-
deep philosophy of the " original goodness and
unlimited perfectibility" of human nature, to
the profounder view of the Hebrew prophets,
the Greek dramatists, Dante's *Divine Comedy*,

Shakespeare's *Hamlet*, Tennyson's *Idylls of
the King*, the great poetry of all lands and
ages, — the clearer, deeper, sadder view, which
sees the mysterious shadow resting on the life
of man, and traces the lines of conflict, disaster,
and death that run through human history,
back to their origin in the gulf which separates
man's moral character from the divine ideal.

*The testi-
mony of
Science.*

Science, with its new theory of evolution,
puts a stern emphasis upon the strength of the
ties which bind man to the brute. It lays bare
the workings of the selfish, sensual, egotistical
impulses in the career of the race. It lengthens
the cords and strengthens the stakes of the
fatal net of heredity which holds all men together in an entanglement of defects of nature
and taints of blood.

"I know of no study," wrote Professor Hux-
ley, "which is so unutterably saddening as that
of the evolution of humanity as set forth in the
annals of history. Out of the darkness of pre-
historic ages man emerges with the marks of his
lowly origin strong upon him. He is a brute,
only more intelligent than the other brutes;
a blind prey to impulses which as often as not
lead him to destruction; a victim to endless
illusions which make his mental existence a
terror and a burden, and fill his physical life

with barren toil and battle. He attains a certain degree of comfort, and develops a more
or less workable theory of life in such favourable
situations as the plains of Mesopotamia or of
Egypt, and then for thousands and thousands
of years struggles with various fortunes, at-
tended by infinite wickedness, bloodshed, and
misery, to maintain himself at this point against
the greed and ambition of his fellow-men. He
makes a point of killing and otherwise persecuting all those who first try to get him to
move on ; and when he has moved a step
farther he foolishly confers post-mortem deifi-
cation on his victims. He exactly repeats the
process with all who want to move a step yet
farther." [1]

This was written by a teacher of science, for
a periodical called *The Nineteenth Century*.
If it had been uttered by a Hebrew prophet, in
the sixth century before Christ, it could not
give a darker picture of human nature.

Modern philosophy is permeated with the *Pessimism*
flavour of pessimism, — the bitter tincture drawn *the tincture of evil.*
from the twisted, tangled roots of sorrowful
perversity which underlie the life of man.

Modern literature is haunted by the persistent spectre of evil, which " will not down."

[1] *The Nineteenth Century*, Feb., 1889. " Agnosticism."

A novel by Zola, or Turgenieff, or Thomas
Hardy, is little more than a commentary on
Jeremiah's text, "The heart is deceitful above
all things, and desperately wicked."[1]

Gloomy as such a view of life is, unmitigated
by any real explanation of its mysterious ail-
ment, unillumined by any hope of its cure,
there is still something wholesome and medici-
nal in it. It is better to know the saddest
truth than to be blinded by the merriest lie.
The sober, stern-browed pessimism which looks
the darkness in the face is sounder and more
heroic than the frivolous, fat-witted optimism
which turns its back, and shuts its eyes, and
laughs.

The folly of ignoring evil. Man, indeed, is framed to live and rise by
hope. But a hope which begins by denying the
facts is a false hope whose path leads upward —
a few steps — to the edge of a precipice of deeper
despair.

The Bridge-Builders in Rudyard Kipling's
story would have been fools if they had tried
to accomplish their work by ignoring the steady
downward thrust of gravitation, or shutting
their eyes to the destructive rage of the Ganges-
flood.

No less foolish is the man who tries to build

[1] Jer. xvii. 9.

a life, or a theory of life, in forgetfulness of the
steady downward thrust of human nature, or in
denial of the reality and universality of the evil
that is in the world.

Hidden it may be; dormant it may be; unrealized it may be in the fulness of its possi-
bilities and powers. The river sleeps in the
smoothness of its flow. The force that draws
all foreheads downward to the dust is checked
and countervailed by other forces. But evil is
always there, a potency of disaster and destruction. All the ills that have been wrought in
the world come from that secret source. In
form they are manifold. In origin and essence
they are one.

II

The Unanswerable Question

The genesis of evil.

How came evil into being?

This is the question which man has always asked, and to which he has never found a perfect answer.

He cannot help asking it, because curiosity, in the nobler sense of the word, is the mainspring of his mind. When man ceases to question he ceases to think.

He cannot find the perfect answer, because his reason is limited and conditioned, and because his intellectual power itself has developed under the shadow, and within the sphere, of the very malign presence which he seeks to account for.

A spirit whose life was beyond the influence of evil might be able to understand and solve the problem of its origin. But even so, it would hardly be possible for such a spirit to communicate this knowledge to other spirits who were born and lived within the domain of evil.

And yet, that man should ask this question, and continue to ask it after thousands of years of baffled thought and disappointed search, is in itself a hopeful and illuminating fact. It

is a question which implies a faith not to be *The ques-*
eradicated, a courage not to be conquered. It *tion of hope.*
speaks of a conviction that evil is not eternal,
but temporal; not sovereign, but subordinate;
not native to the universe, but a foreigner and
an intruder. It testifies to man's knowledge
that evil is not the whole, but a part; not the
straight line, but the deflection; not a necessary element in the perfect harmony of being,
but a false note which breaks the chord.

If man should ask, "How came good into
being?" he would be in the region of despair.
While he continues to ask, "How came evil
into being?" he is in the region of hope.

All the answers to this question which have
been attempted, may be classified under three
forms. The first amounts to a denial of the
existence of evil. The second destroys the reality of the distinction between evil and good.
The third confesses that the primal origin of
evil is a mystery, and bids us rest content with
a knowledge of its reality and its mode of manifestation in the world.

All theories which are based upon the idea of *Is evil*
the essential *nothingness* of evil, amount to a *nothing?*
practical denial of its existence. Traces of
such theories may be found even in Christian

writers. A theologian as orthodox as Thomas Aquinas has said, "God created everything that exists; but sin is *nothing;* so God was not the author of it." In Robert Browning's poem of *Abt Vogler*, the idea is put into a single verse.

"The evil is naught, is null, is silence implying sound."

Darkness is but the absence of light. Evil is but the negation of good.

The rock upon which all these negative theories go to pieces is the practical conviction that evil is just as real to us in our experience, just as solid, just as operative, as good is. The desire which seeks a wrong pleasure is no less vivid than that which seeks a right pleasure. The will which determines a wicked action is just as strong as that which determines a righteous action. The end sought is no more negative in one case than it is in the other. If evil is a nothing, it is a strangely active, positive, and potent nothing, with all the qualities of a something. The theories which attempt to account for its origin by tracing it to a mere negation or absence of good, raise a harder question than that which they attempt to answer. Instead of asking how evil came

into being, we must ask, How did evil, which
is a mere nothing, come to have the reality,
the life, and the power of a something?

All theories which are based upon the idea of *Is evil*
the *necessity* of evil lead to a practical denial *necessary?*
of the distinction between evil and good. For
if the necessity be purely natural, that is to
say materialistic, then there is no possible
ground for making such a distinction. The
inexplicable constitution of the original atoms
of the universe has produced mother's love and
murderer's hate in precisely the same way, and
the one is as good, or as evil, as the other.
But if the necessity be ordained by any kind of
a Divine Being, then all its results must be
according to His will and must serve His purpose. Any essential difference between the
evil and the good becomes unimaginable. All
that is left is a formal difference, in which evil
is good in disguise, a necessary but unrecognized
element in the development of the world. We
must accept the statement of Pope's *Essay on
Man:*

> " All nature is but art, unknown to thee;
>   All chance, direction which thou canst not see;
>   All discord, harmony not understood;
>   All partial evil, universal good;

And spite of pride, in erring reason's spite,
One truth is clear, Whatever is, is right."

The "ought not."   The rock upon which these theories of the necessity of evil go to pieces is the practical knowledge of the nature of evil, which comes to us through the same moral sense which makes us aware of its existence. There is absolutely no variation in the testimony of human consciousness on this point. Evil is recognized not merely as something which is, but also as something which " ought not to be." This is the mark by which we know it. If from this mark we set out to trace its origin to a divine necessity which has ordained it and called it into being to serve a good purpose, then we must admit that our original mark of evil is an illusion, a false label. It is not "that which ought not to be." It is "that which ought to be." The whole problem of the origin of evil dissolves into an absurdity. We are left to face a still harder question. How did our moral consciousness, with such an error at the very heart of it, come into being ? Is it a mistake ? Or is it a lie ? Or is it perhaps a divinely imposed delusion ? [1]

[1] Schleiermacher and Ritschl, among theologians, present a theory of the sense of guilt as a purely subjective feeling,

But if our common sense turns away from
these theories of evil as originating in nothingness, or in necessity, in what direction shall we
look for an answer to the question of how it
came into being?   There is only one line left
open; and that is the line of the facts as they
lie before us in the world of experience. This
is the line that we must take. We must hold
to it firmly. We must follow it as far as we
can; and when we can follow it no farther we
must stop, sure that to turn aside from that
line is to fall into falsehood.

*The true
line of
inquiry.*

What, then, are the facts of evil recognized
by the moral sense of mankind? First of all,
that it is "that which ought not to be."   Then,
that it actually is.   Then, that it manifests
itself in our own experience in connection with
voluntary acts, — acts of choice, or acts of compliance, — contrary to "that which ought to be."
But "that which ought to be," must be the will
of God.   Therefore "that which ought not to
be," can only make itself known in the world
through the will of a creature capable of going
contrary to God.   The possibility of evil depends upon the liberty of the created will.
Liberty, then, which means the power of con-

*Three facts
of evil.*

which makes it amount, in effect, to a result of ignorance,
or an illusion ordained by God for a good end.

trary choice, must be the door through which evil entered the world.[1]

But what lies behind that door? From what secret region does the evil that passes through it draw its birth and its power? Why does it enter in? Why does God permit it? Here we stand face to face with the impenetrable mystery.

Certainly God as creator must have bestowed the gift of liberty with a good purpose. He must have intended man to choose the good in order to attain real and permanent freedom; that is, the power of self-realization in harmony with the ideal of his nature. But when evil comes in through liberty, the purpose of liberty is violated, the very end of its being is frustrated. The will, choosing evil, comes into subjection to it, and cannot realize itself in a lasting freedom of concord with good.

Evil, then, as it manifests itself in the world, is a purposeless, aimless thing. It is an abuse of the power of choice. It is caprice. It is violence to reason. We can give no rational explanation of its origin, because its origin appears irrational. It is incomprehensible. There is a madness about it which confuses the mind. The Greeks took refuge from it

[1] *The Gospel for an Age of Doubt*, ch. vi., "Liberty."

in their myth of Atë, "the eldest daughter of Zeus, the power of bane, who blindeth all." But this was only a shift of desperate ignorance to get rid of the difficulty by transferring it from the human to the divine.

A wiser, humbler, more reverent thought *It does not* holds fast to the conviction that wherever the *come from* *God.* madness of evil comes from, it does not come from God. Its origin is beyond our ken. "Evil is the inscrutable mystery of the world; it ever remains, in its inmost depths, impenetrable darkness." [1] It is not to be comprehended in its cause. It is to be known in its effects, which are symptoms of its nature.

This is the point to which our line leads us, *Its birth-* and here it leaves us. To go farther is to *place* *hidden.* abandon fact for fancy. Christianity itself does not profess to give us light beyond this point. It presents no doctrine of the origin of evil. It tells us only how it came into the world, and what it means in the life of man. Where it came from is unrevealed.

There are two places in the Bible where the *Adam* entrance of evil and the fall of man are de- *and the* *Prodigal.* scribed — and they both teach the same lesson. Christ's parable of the Prodigal Son [2] is just as

[1] Müller, *On the Christian Doctrine of Sin*, II., p. 174.
[2] Luke xv.

true, just as significant, as the story of Adam's lost Paradise.[1] In both stories the birthplace of the evil is hidden.   The serpent that tempted Eve, and the far country that allured the Prodigal, are symbols of a mystery.   In both stories the entrance of the evil is through self-will — blind, perverse, ruinous, but free, and therefore responsible.   In both stories the nature of the evil is rebellion, self-injury, separation from God.[2]   In both stories the result of the evil in man's heart is the sense of sin.

Adam's story stops there; but the Prodigal's story goes on to salvation.

[1] Gen. iii.
[2] *The Gospel for an Age of Doubt*, pp. 266 ff.

III

The Sense of Sin

The sense of sin is something deeper than the *Sin is an interpreta-* consciousness of evil.[1] Evil is a broad, vague *tion of evil.* word. It covers all that ought not to be, but it does not make clear the nature of the " ought not." It is a general description of that which prevents perfection, destroys happiness, produces discord and misery.

Sin is a precise, sharp word. It translates the idea of evil from the language of philosophy into the language of religion. It defines the nature of the " ought not " as resting on a divine law. It recognizes the presence and the guilt of a contrary will in disobedience to that law. It interprets the nature and the consequence of evil in the light that comes from God.

The consciousness of evil is universal. There *The unrest* is a feeling of conflict, of disorder, of moral *of mankind.* perturbation and unrest, diffused through all humanity. This is the great mark of division between the life of man and the life of nature. Emerson has described it in his poem of *The*

[1] Fairbairn, *The Place of Christ in Modern Theology,* p. 452.

Sphinx.   Nature is harmonious, joyful, unconscious of strife between the real and the
ideal.

> "But man crouches and blushes,
>   Absconds and conceals;
> He creepeth and peepeth,
>   He palters and steals;
> Infirm, melancholy,
>   Jealous glancing around,
> An oaf, an accomplice,
>   He poisons the ground.
>
> "Out spoke the great mother,
>   Beholding his fear; —
> At the sound of her accents
>   Cold shuddered the sphere;
> 'Who has drugged my boy's cup?
>   Who has mixed my boy's bread?
> Who, with sadness and madness,
>   Has turned my child's head?'"

Conscience.   This mysterious unrest, this vague trouble,
this nameless, haunting distress, is an utterance of man's consciousness that he belongs
to another world from that which is ruled
by mere necessity.   It is an instinctive confession that beyond the power of control, to
which all physical life is subject, he feels a
power of command, to which his spiritual life
ought to be subject.   This power of command
makes itself known to him through conscience,
which is the power of perceiving the differ-

ence between the " ought to be " and **the**
" ought not to be."

" Whom do you count the worst man upon
earth ? " says Robert Browning in *Christmas
Eve.*

> " Be sure that he knows, in his conscience, more
>   Of what right is, than arrives at birth
>   In the best man's acts that we bow before :
>   This last knows better — true, but my fact is,
>   'Tis one thing to know, and another to practise."

This contrast between knowledge and practice is the root. of the consciousness of evil,
whose symptoms are unrest, shame, and fear.

> " Thus conscience doth make cowards of us all."

It is a feeling of resistance to a moral pres-
sure, of disobedience to a commanding power,
of discord with a dim ideal. But it is also a
sense of compliance with an inward impulse, of
obedience to a native desire, of agreement with
a secret passion.

It is not altogether dark. It could not exist *The light*
in a world where there was nothing but evil. *behind con-*
science.
In a universe wholly material there could be
no materialism. In a race utterly and totally
evil there could be no consciousness of evil.

Neither could it exist in a world where separate evils stood alone and had no common

ground in human nature. Each misdeed would then be a miracle. It would be a rootless, unrecognizable, nameless thing. Conscience perceives evil not only in its individuality, but also in its solidarity. When a man does wrong he feels that he is a partner in a great conspiracy, a sharer, by choice or by compliance, in a widespread rebellion.

"There is in man," wrote Frederic Amiel in his diary, "an instinct of revolt, an enemy of all law, a rebel which will stoop to no yoke, not even that of reason, duty, and wisdom. This element in us is the root of all sin—*das radicale Böse* of Kant."[1]

Ithuriel's spear.

But this feeling of radical evil and of its presence and potency in every misdeed, needs more light to make its meaning clear. Evil is known as sin only when good is known as the will and command and ideal of a personal and holy God.

This is what St. Paul teaches. Revelation is given to make clear the nature of the gulf between man as he is and man as he ought to be. Evil is not a step in a progress toward the ideal. It is a chasm which cuts us off from the ideal. The reason why it cuts us off is because it is contrary to God's will, through

[1] Amiel's *Journal*, 23d Feb., 1870, Vol. II., p. 55.

which alone the ideal can be realized. The moral law reveals that will to us as positive, personal, righteous, and immutable. The law enters that the offence may abound, for "by the law is the knowledge of sin."[1]

The sense of sin, therefore, is a step beyond the consciousness of evil. And it is a step toward light.

It is the interpretation of evil as an offence against God, a disobedience to God, a separation from God. It comes into being only with Theism, the faith in a holy, wise, and righteous Spirit as creator of the world. It is not until this light breaks upon the soul that Amiel's words become true : "All men long to recover a lost harmony with the great order of things, and to feel themselves approved and blessed by the author of the Universe. All know what suffering is, and long for happiness. All know what sin is, and feel the need of pardon." *Sin against God.*

Religion must begin, then, — even if we hold that its ultimate aim is the deliverance of men from evil, — religion must begin not with a doctrine of evil, but with a doctrine of God.[2]

Its keynote must be the first article of the

---

[1] Rom. iii. 20 ; v. 20.
[2] *The Gospel for an Age of Doubt*, Preface to 6th ed.

D

creed, "I believe in God, the Father Almighty, maker of heaven and earth." When He is hidden, forgotten, denied, the gospel for an age of doubt must prepare the way for the gospel for a world of sin. Over the vague unrest, the inarticulate shame, the uncomprehended fear, of an evil world, the light of God's love and God's law must be poured. Thus only can the evil doer find his way to that place of penitence, where he cries, "Against thee, thee only, have I sinned, and done this evil in thy sight." [1]

The light beyond the law.

The sense of sin, therefore, is not by any means a hopeless thing. It is an evidence of life, in its very pain; of enlightenment, in its very shame; of nearness to God, in its very humiliation before Him.

There is a passage in a recent story of human life that puts the truth very simply and beautifully. [2] A woman that was a sinner has come to a minister of Christ to confess her sin. The old man speaks to her as she kneels at his feet, weeping.

"You have sinned, and suffered for your sin. You have asked your Heavenly Father to forgive you, and He has forgiven you. But still

[1] Psalm li. 4.
[2] Margaret Deland, *Old Chester Tales*, p. 84.

you suffer. Woman, be thankful that you can suffer. The worst trouble in the world is the trouble that does not know God, and so does not suffer. Without such knowledge there is no suffering. The sense of sin in the soul is the apprehension of Almighty God."

IV

The Hopeful Fear

Sin a mystery.

Sin is not a thing to be defined. It is a thing to be felt. Every attempt at a definition comes short of the reality. If it is insisted upon as the full truth, it becomes a guide to error. Every genuine feeling of sin throws some light upon the reality and helps us to perceive that which we can never explain.

One of the inexplicable elements of sin is the connection between its root in the race and its fruits in the individual. We cannot explain how it is that each man should feel himself free enough to be fully responsible for his own evil thoughts and feelings and actions, and yet conscious at the same time that they are joined to a common ground of evil in human nature. Stranger still is the fact that this propensity to evil is felt to be not an excuse but an aggravation. The man who injures his brother in a fit of passion, takes no comfort in the remembrance of his anger. The anger itself is part of his condemnation. Who ever excused a foul deed, to his own conscience, with the saying that he had a foul nature? Sin is not only an act: it is a condition, a state; and separate sins are not better, they are worse, because they spring from a common root. "It is of sin," says Boetius, "that we do not love that which is best."

Christ taught the truth of original sin. He did not explain it, but He declared it when He said, "Out of the heart proceed evil thoughts, murders, adulteries, fornications, thefts, false witness, blasphemies."[1] Side by side with this truth He proclaimed the guilt of actual sin when He said, "Whosoever looketh on a woman to lust after her hath committed adultery with her already in his heart."[2] He taught also that all men need to be delivered from both original and actual sin when He said, "Ye must be born again,"[3] and "Except ye repent ye shall all likewise perish."[4] But when His disciples pressed Him to explain this mystery of the connection between the root and the fruit of evil, with their question, "Lord, who did sin, this man or his parents, that he was born blind?" Christ refused to answer them. He said, "Neither did this man sin nor his parents" (that is, in relation to the point of their question), "but that the works of God might be made manifest in him."[5]

Original sin makes originality in sins impos-

Original sin.

---

[1] Matt. xv. 19.   [2] Matt. v. 28.
[3] John iii. 7.   [4] Luke xiii. 3.   [5] John ix. 2, 3.

sible.   There is a fatal resemblance and rela-
tionship in all the evils that are done under
the sun, from the days before the flood even
until now.

And yet every sin originates in the heart that
commits it.   Each individual will that consents
to evil chooses for itself.   The ground of this
choice is hidden in darkness.   It may lie in a
region beyond the sphere of time and space, an
antenatal state.[1]

Every sin a
fall of man.
But the operation of this choice is manifest
in the light.   Every sin is a fall of man.

To be really conscious of a single sin is to
feel its secret connections and infinite possibili-
ties.   It is to catch sight of the bottomless
gulf and have a sense of the immeasurable
peril of walking beside it with unguarded
feet.

In Goethe's *Confessions of a Beautiful*
Soul there is a singular and searching passage which goes very deep into human experience.

"For more than a year," — so runs the confession, — "I was forced to feel that if an unseen Hand had not protected me, I might have
become a Girard, a Cartouche, a Damiens, or

[1] Coleridge, *Aids to Reflection*, pp. 268 ff.; Müller, *On the*
Christian Doctrine of Sin, II., pp. 357 ff.

almost any moral monster that one can name.
I felt the predisposition to it in my heart.
God, what a discovery!"[1]

John Bunyan's exclamation, when he looked
from his window at a condemned malefactor
going to execution, — "There goes John Bunyan, but for the grace of God," — has found an
echo in many a heart.   But this echo is not a
defence; it is a confession.

The sense of sin covers character as well as *Sinful*
deeds.   It clings not only to what we have *character.*
done, but also to what we are prone to do.
It was in this region below the surface that
Jesus touched and exposed it, with His searching tenderness, His holy insight, His relentless
love.   Not only His word, piercing like an
arrow of light to the roots of evil in pride
and selfishness and lust and greed and hypoc-
risy, but also His life, in its stainless purity
and flawless truth, was an infallible detective
of the furtive evil seeking to hide itself, like
Adam and Eve in the story of Eden, among
the trees of the garden.   It was for this reason that the Scribes and Pharisees hated Him,
because He made them hate themselves.   It
was for this reason that Peter feared to be
with Him, and cried, "Depart from me, for

[1] *Wilhelm Meister's Lehrjahre*, Part II., p. 112.

I am a sinful man, O Lord." [1]   It was for this
reason that the woman of the city streets drew
close to Him, and bathed His feet with her
tears, because she knew that He knew that she
was a sinner. [2]

There are four elements in a true sense of
sin: shame, pain, fear, and hope.

The shame in sin.   The shame comes from its ugliness, its defilement, its marring and mocking of those ele-
ments in us which we feel belong to the divine
image and our better nature.   No man is born
without an ideal.

> "Take all in a word: the truth in God's breast,
>   Lies trace for trace upon ours impressed :
>   Though He is so bright, and we so dim,
>   We are made in His image to witness Him." [3]

The failure to be true to this ideal, the be-
fouling and breaking of this image, is the
shame of sin.

The pain in sin.   The pain comes from its enslaving and imprisoning power.   Man was made for liberty.
But sin is bondage to evil.   "Whoso com-
mitteth sin is the servant of sin." [4]   The conflict within our members, the law of the flesh

---

[1] Luke v. 8.   [3] Browning, *Christmas Eve*, xvii.
[2] Luke vii. 38.   [4] John viii. 34.

warring against the law of the spirit, the weight
of the chains of evil habit, the tyranny of
sensual lusts and passions, — these make the
misery of human life. Stevenson's parable of
Dr. Jekyll and Mr. Hyde is a commentary
on the seventh chapter of the Epistle to the
Romans.

> " The gods are just, and of our pleasant vices
>   Make instruments to plague us."

"Crime and punishment," says Emerson,
"grow out of one stem. Punishment is a
fruit that, unsuspected, ripens within the flower
that concealed it."

The fear comes from the sense of disobedi- *The fear in sin.*
ence to a high, mysterious, inexorable com-
mand. It is not possible to feel sin without
fear, except by denying the existence of all
moral law. As a matter of fact, the consciousness of evil has always carried with it
in all human experience a feeling of secret
apprehension, a troubled expectation and dread
of punishment. Fear is related to guilt as
personality is related to law. The reality of
the one relation carries with it the reality of
the other. Here we come face to face with a
crucial question in religion.

Is there anything objective and actual which

corresponds to this human element of fear in the sense of sin? Is there anything for sinful man to be afraid of?

Certainly there must be, unless the whole testimony of our moral nature is an illusion. The condemnation of sin rests not merely upon the feeling that sin is self-injury, self-mutilation, but upon the deeper sense that it is an offence against a law outside of us, and above us, and justly sovereign over us.[1] Such a law must have within itself the right, the power, the inexorable necessity of punishment. Resting upon the will, and expressing the character of a righteous God, the ruler of the universe, it implies in Him a holy indignation against all that breaks and dishonours it.

"For consider," says one of the greatest preachers whose voice has been heard in the nineteenth century, "sin violates and defies the Moral Law of God. And what is God's Moral Law? Is it a law which, like the laws of nature, as we call them, might conceivably have been other than it is? Certainly not. We can conceive much in nature being very different from what it is — suns and stars moving in smaller cycles; men and animals in different shapes; the chemistry, the geology,

[1] *Lux Mundi*, p. 277.

the governing rules of the material universe,
quite unlike what they actually are. God's
liberty in creating physical beings was in no
way limited by His own laws, whether of force
or of matter. But can we, if we believe in a
Moral God, conceive Him saying, 'Thou mayest
lie,' 'Thou mayest do murder'? . . . **The**
Moral Law is not a code which He might have
made other than it is ; it is His own Moral
Nature, thrown into a shape which makes it
intelligible and applicable to us His creatures ;
and therefore in violating it we are opposing,
not something which He has made, but might
have made otherwise, like the laws of nature,—
but Himself. Sin, if it could, would destroy
God." [1]

The penalty of sin under moral law is not *The penalty.*
less certain, but more certain, than the penalty
of disobedience to natural law. The wholesome fear which makes a burnt child dread the
fire is no more trustworthy than the salutary
fear which makes a sinful man dread the divine
indignation. Both are premonitions of an
actual peril, safeguards against a real danger.
But the latter, if Christ knew the truth, is far
more needful, far more terrible. For he said :
" Be not afraid of them that kill the body, and

[1] Henry Parry Liddon, *Passiontide Sermons*, p. 296.

after that have no more than they can do.
But I will forewarn you whom ye shall fear:
Fear him, which after he hath killed, hath
power to cast into hell; yea, I say unto you,
fear him."[1]   And this He said, not unto His
enemies to terrify them, but unto His friends
to warn and save them.

The wrath of God.   The fear that lurks in sin is not an illusion.
It is an admonition.   It corresponds to some-
thing real outside of us.   And that something
is the reality which religion calls "the wrath
of God."

It is inconceivable that this holy wrath should
be perfectly comprehended or explained by us.
It is equally inconceivable that it should be
doubted or denied.   A righteous judge incapa-
ble of indignation against crime would be unfit
to sit in the seat of justice.   A holy God in-
capable of wrath against sin would be disquali-
fied to rule the world.

There must be a moral necessity in God which
calls for the condemnation of evil as sin.   This
necessity comes from every side of His nature,
—from His justice first, but also from His
purity, His wisdom, His goodness, His love.
And the condemnation expresses every side of
His relation to the world.   As Creator, He dis-

[1] Luke xii. 5.

approves the marring of the ideal. As Judge,
He condemns the transgression of the law. As
Lord, He resents and reproves treason and rebel-
lion against His government. As Father, He
is wounded and offended by ingratitude against
His love and separation from His fellowship.
All these holy perfections are included and im-
plied in that mysterious reality of which the
Scripture speaks as " the wrath of God, coming
upon the children of disobedience." [1]

But there is a form in which this truth of *A false*
the divine wrath has been presented which *doctrine.*
makes it utterly hateful, and, indeed, incredible. It is the form which forgets and denies
those perfections of God out of· which His
indignation proceeds. It is the form which
introduces sin itself into the very heart of
God's feeling against sin. It is the form which
makes Him fierce, vindictive, implacable, and
cruel.

To defame and dishonour the divine wrath
is worse than to doubt or deny it.

To separate God's indignation against sin
from His love toward man is to blaspheme His
name.

This is the fault of which, alas, human theology has too often been guilty, — a fault which

[1] Eph. v. 6.

has brought its own deep punishment in the revolt of human nature against the hideous misrepresentation of religion. Take two examples of this black caricature of God's feeling toward sin, from the writings of Robert South, one of the most eloquent and eminent preachers of the seventeenth century.

God slandered. "The same relation of a Creator that endears God to the innocent, fires Him against a sinner. God looks upon the soul as Amnon did upon Tamar : while it was a virgin He loved it ; but now it is deflowered he hates it."

"A physician has a servant ; while this servant lives honestly with him he is fit to be used and to be employed in his occasions ; but if this servant should commit a felony and for that be condemned, he can then be actively serviceable to him no longer ; he is fit only for him to dissect, and make an object upon which to show the experiments of his skill. So while man was yet innocent he was fit to be used by God in a way of active obedience ; but now having sinned, and being sentenced by the law to death as a malefactor, he is a fit matter only for God to torment and show the wonders of His vindictive justice."

The world is to be congratulated that such teaching as this has become obsolete and incredible. Whatever system of theology it may have belonged to, is now as dead as Dagon. A God who had any resemblance in His character to that vilest and most despicable sinner, Amnon, a God who could use His children, even after they had disobeyed Him, as "fit matter to torment and show the wonders of His vindictive justice," would be a nightmare horror of moral monstrosity, infinitely worse than no God at all. To worship such a God would be to worship an omnipotent devil.

God cannot be angry, even against sin, as sinful men are angry, because in Him there is no sin. Whatever His holy wrath against evil may mean, it certainly must be eternally consistent with His purity, His goodness, His compassion, and His love. *God's wrath as pure as His love.*

Therefore, the true fear which is an element in the sense of sin, — the fear which is simply seeing what evil is, what judgment is, what law is, and what punishment is, — the fear which is reverent, sober, steadying, stimulating, healthful, — the fear which gives depth and grandeur to our conception of the world and enters mightily into every serious and noble life, — the fear which is not spiritual cowardice, but an incitement to courage, not abject superstition, but a reasonable awe, —

the fear which comes upon every sinful soul as an influence of quickening intelligence, a powerful movement of imperilled life, in the presence of the just and holy God,— this fear carries in its heart a secret and imperishable hope.

The prodigal says, Father.
The hope that dwells in the sense of sin! Strange mystery of the deepest of all sorrows,— seed of light hidden in the womb of darkness, — indomitable testimony of the lost soul to its faith that some one is seeking for it in the wilderness!

Sin is the separation of man from God.

The sense of sin is God's unbroken hold upon the heart of man.

The sacrifices on myriad altars bear witness to .it. The prayers of penitence rising from all dark corners of the earth bear witness to it. The tremulous homeward-turnings of innumerable souls from far countries of misery and loneliness bear witness to it.

"Father, I have sinned against heaven and in thy sight, and am no more worthy to be called thy son!"

But mark,— he still says, *Father!*

III

THE BIBLE WITHOUT CHRIST

But were he man,
And death ends all; then was that tortured death
On Calvary a thing to make the pulse
Of memory quail and stop.

—Richard Watson Gilder, *In Palestine.*

THE BIBLE WITHOUT CHRIST

THE Bible, if indeed it be the true text-book *What we* of religion, must contain the answer to man's *need in the Bible.* cry as a sinner to God as a Saviour. It must disclose to man a remedy for the pain, a consolation for the shame, a rescue from the fear, and a confirmation of the secret hope, that he dimly and confusedly feels in the sense of sin. A Bible with no message of deliverance from sin would be a useless luxury in a sinful world. It would lack that quality of perfect fitness to human need which is one of the most luminous evidences of a divine word. The presence of a clear message of salvation is an essential element in the proof of inspiration.

That there is such a message of salvation in *The word of* the Bible, no intelligent reader can deny. That *hope centres in Christ.* it centres in Christ, is what this chapter is intended to show.

Jesus Himself took this view of the Scriptures. To the unbelieving Jews, who trusted in their sacred books but felt no need of Him,

He said, "Search the Scriptures; for in these ye think ye have eternal life : and they are they which testify of me."[1]

What would it be without Him? Suppose for a moment that this were a mistake. Suppose that there were no testimonies to Christ in the Old Testament, no promises of His coming, no foreshadowings of His saving mission and power, — only law and ritual, poetry and history, philosophy and prophecy.

Suppose also that the New Testament contained nothing but the record of the moral teachings of Jesus and His followers, without reference to His life and death as a visible revelation of divine justice and mercy in personality and action. Suppose that it had not a word to say about His work in relation to men as sinners. Suppose, in short, that it gave the words of Jesus about the reality and nature and guilt of sin, about the pain and shame and fear of humanity, but no explanation of Him, no recognition of what He did and suffered, no view of His crucifixion and resurrection, in their bearing upon the sin of the world.

Suppose the Bible without Christ. What hope of salvation would it contain? What would it be worth to us? What would be left of it as the divine answer to the need of a sinful world?

[1] John v. 39.

In the Old Testament, with its partial and imperfect vision of the nature of evil, an unbroken shadow.

In the New Testament, with its poignant disclosure of the secret of sin, an intolerable light.

We can never realize the true meaning and value of this book of the world's hope until we try the experiment of reading it without the message which makes it hopeful. How the Bible centres in Christ can be learned best by trying to take Christ out of the Bible.

The experiment.

I

The Unbroken Shadow

The pictures of Genesis. The Old Testament does not begin with a theory of the nature of God and the origin of evil. It begins with a picture of ˙creation, followed immediately by a picture of the entrance of evil into the world, and from this point it unrolls a graphic panorama of human life.

Some people interpret this panorama of Genesis as a series of scientific diagrams. Others interpret it as a series of poetic illustrations. It makes little difference in regard to their value for purposes of spiritual instruction. Upon the whole, the vital truths by which the souls of men live, have been conveyed in poetic illustrations rather more frequently and fully than in scientific diagrams. Dante's *Divine Comedy* has taught more than Euclid's *Geometry*.

The vision and the background. One thing is clear in the book of Genesis. By whatever method we translate its records, their meaning is the same. They show a vision of human sin, conflict, and suffering, against a divine background of offended love, righteous indignation, and just retribution.

This view of human life corresponds very closely with what we know of it from other sources.

Unruly appetite, lustful passion, envy and discord, violence and terror and guilt, are written as clearly in the story of the beginnings of all tribes and nations and families, as in the story of Adam and Eve, Cain and Abel, Noah, Abraham, and Jacob.

It is difficult to conceive how a pure and righteous God could look upon such a race, made in His own image, with dominion over the creatures, and with capacities of infinite development in wisdom and virtue and power, yet descending to lower depths of animalism than the very beasts of the field, developing passions more cruel and treacherous and base than those of the brute creation, — upon such a race it is impossible that God should look without repulsion and holy wrath. Not wrath as we know it, always tainted with selfishness, but wrath as only God can know it, absolutely unselfish and springing out of frustrated benevolence. The more He loves men and women, the more He must hate the evil which mars His image in their characters and defeats His design in their lives.

God hates sin because He loves man.

Now take away out of these pictures which

*The ray of
light ob-
scured.*

are given in Genesis, that one ray of light
which flashes in the Messianic promise that the
seed of the woman shall bruise the serpent's
head,[1] that one thread of gold which runs from
this promise through the lives of those who
believe in God, keeping them in touch with
Him, making them His faithful seed, because
from them there is to come a star, a sceptre, a
Shiloh unto whom the nations shall be gathered,[2]
— take away that ray of light, that thread of
gold, and what remains? Sin and shame and
struggle below; baffled love, frustrated benevolence, inevitable condemnation above. The
expulsion from Eden — the thorn-cursed soil
— the brand on the brow of Cain — the shat-
tered Babel — the whelming flood — the fiery
tempest on Sodom and Gomorrah — wars and
disasters, tumults and captivities — man a rebellious, wretched, wandering creature — God
justly offended at the violation of His law — a
sin-twisted, suffering, fearful world below — a
stainless, silent heaven above, — and no bridge
across the gulf.

Sinai.

Now turn to the law given through Moses.
His part in history was twofold. He was
the leader of the Exodus; and that means

[1] Gen. iii. 15.   [2] Gen. xlix. 10.

emancipation from human tyranny. He was the explorer of Sinai; and that means subjugation to divine justice.

Alpine climbers reckon their glory by the conquest of virgin peaks of snow and ice. Moses made the first ascent of a virgin peak of fire and smoke. The landscape that he saw from that summit was ringed by the horizon of immutable law.

Moses talked with God face to face. But there was a frown upon the divine countenance, and the voice which spoke to him was as stern as fate. The people heard it only as the voice of a trumpet, mysterious and inarticulate, whereat they did exceedingly fear and quake, and entreated that it should not be spoken unto them any more. But Moses heard the words, and knew that they were inevitable and eternal.

Ten commandments he brought down from the mount, written out clearly so that all men should understand them, and on stone so that they should endure to all generations. One of the commandments was positive. Nine of them were negative. Moses was the divine prohibitionist. Nine-tenths of his emphasis lies on the "Thou shalt not."

"Thou shalt not."

But the point that pierces us, in this revela-

"But I will."

tion through Moses, is that every "Thou shalt not" is a disclosure of what men have done, and are prone to do, and would like to do again if they dared. The commandments sound like a shouting from the mountain-top of the secrets of many hearts. After each divine word which says, "Thou shalt not," follows a human murmur which says, "But I will."

The history of Israel.

A Bible was once published in which, by a typographical error, the *not* was omitted from the seventh commandment. It was called "the wicked Bible." The history of Israel, starting from Sinai, reads like a commentary on a wicked Bible with the printer's error multiplied by ten. Carry the commandments through the books of the Judges and the Kings, and you must acknowledge that they compel the conclusion that man is what he ought not to be, and ought not to be what he is.

The bright spot hidden.

The one bright spot in the law given by Moses is the commandment to make a mercy-seat in the Tabernacle, where the sins of the people may be confessed before Almighty God,[1] and where the blood of sacrifice, sprinkled upon the Ark, may symbolize an atonement between man and God. The one good hope which cheered Moses in his ministry to a disobedient

[1] Ex. xxv. ; Lev. xvi.

and gainsaying folk, was the promise that God
would raise up a prophet from among his brethren unto whom the people should hearken.[1]
Blot out that prediction of Christ, and Moses
stands as an embodiment of failure, — a leader
who emancipated the nation and condemned the
race, — the messenger of a divine law which
was broken even while he was carrying it down
from the burning mount.

Turn from history and law to poetry and *The music*
experience.   In the Psalms the thunders of *of Psalms.*
Sinai are set to music and translated into
song.

But what is that song?   It is the song of
the unattainable.   It is the lyric utterance of
desire and disappointment, shame and penitence.   Those broken-hearted Psalms !   How
they ring the changes on human frailty and
suffering and remorse !   How sad and searching the light with which they are illuminated
in the story of David's life !

He could sing divinely, but he could **not**
live as he sang.

Sin is the shadow on genius.

Literature full of beauty and harmony : life *The discord*
full of ugliness and discord.   A book written *of life.*

[1] Deut. xviii. 15.

with simplicity and purity and noble sentiment: a writer touched with vanity and selfishness, impurity and vengeful passion. How
often has that strange contrast been discovered!

David knew his own infirmity and guilt.
He knew the corruption and disgrace of his
house. He laid hold on the promise of divine
mercy in the Christ. He looked and longed
for the coming of that King who should reign
in righteousness forever. He did not understand the full meaning of that hope. He held
fast to it as a drowning man clings to a rope in
the night. He does not see it. He feels it.

The gleam of mercy lost. Take away that rescuing hope of divine help
laid upon one who is mighty to save,[1] and what
is left in the Psalms? A passion of longing
for inaccessible holiness.

> "The desire of the moth for the star,
>   Of the night for the morrow;
> The devotion to something afar
>   From the sphere of our sorrow."

The poetry of the Bible without Christ is a
musical confession of the impossibility of getting out of God's sight, and of the hopelessness
of being pure enough in heart to have sight
of God.

[1] Psalm lxxxix. 19.

Does the philosophy of the Bible bring us *Solomon's wisdom.* any different message, apart from Christ?

Solomon stands in the Old Testament as the representative of wisdom. In the books that bear his name the divine commandments are cut and polished into the jewels of an ethical system. They become brilliant, symmetrical, memorable; compact treasures of morality, fit to keep — in a storehouse.

A hundred epigrams flash from the divine law, in the hands of Solomon, like rays of light. Its wisdom, reasonableness, and beauty are exhibited from every side. We see how prudent, how profitable, how admirable it is to be perfectly good, — and how impossible!

The king who made these diamond proverbs *Solomon's folly.* was the man who showed us how easily they may be burned to coal in the flame of passion.

The eleventh chapter of the First Book of Kings is the record of an experiment in the reduction of philosophy to ashes. The lover of wisdom chooses folly for his bed-fellow. The sage whose shining words rise like an airy ladder toward the skies, finds, like other men, that the downward path is the easiest. The wisest of mankind, in theory, becomes the meanest, in practice, — an idolater despising idols, a sensualist praising virtue, a tyrant extolling justice, an unchained prisoner of his own despair.

Solomon's epitaph. The book of Ecclesiastes, whoever wrote it, contains the epitaph of Solomon. " Vanity of vanities, all is vanity." It is the hand-book of pessimists ; the tragic monodrama of man's self-betrayal ; the epic of the suicide of hope. Close the book, and write upon it this sentence, "The world by wisdom knew not God."[1]

The mount of prophecy. Beyond philosophy rises prophecy, — the mount of vision, whose top touches the stars and whose horizon spreads beyond the encircling ocean-stream of time.

The human name that is graven highest on this mountain is the name of Isaiah. Whether that name represents the prophetic elevation of only one among the sons of men, or of more than one, matters little to us in our present study. The Isaiah-spirit is the same, whether the mount was climbed but once, or more than once. The loftiest point reached in the Old Testament is that at which we see, in lonely grandeur, a human figure called Isaiah.

There he stands, above the confusions and perturbations, the wrecked hopes, and the on-rushing calamities, the shames and fears, the

[1] 1 Cor. i. 21.

desolations and disasters of his people. He
looks around him, with unsealed eyes, and what
is it that he beholds?

He sees " one that cometh from Edom, with *Isaiah's hope.*
dyed garments from Bozrah, glorious in his
apparel, travelling in the greatness of his
strength, speaking in righteousness, mighty
to save."[1] But this vision, if there is no Christ
in the Old Testament, is a delusion, a mirage,
a Brocken-spectre. It vanishes. And what is
left?

An unbroken shadow of disgrace, despair, *The residue of despair.*
and gloom, resting like night upon the world.
" Ah sinful nation, a people laden with iniquity, a seed of evil doers, children that are cor-
rupters: they have forsaken the Lord, they have
provoked the Holy One of Israel unto anger,
they are gone away backward."[2] Burden after
burden, in the prophet's song, — the burden
of Babylon, the burden of Moab, the burden
of Damascus, the burden of Egypt. Doom
after doom, around the prophet's horizon, — the
doom of Israel, the doom of Judah. " The
whole head is sick, and the whole heart faint.
From the sole of the foot even unto the head
there is no soundness in it; but wounds, and
bruises, and putrifying sores."[3]

[1] Is. lxiii. 1.   [2] Is. i. 4.   [3] Is. i. 5, 6.

*The world's
want.*
Never man lived on earth who felt so deeply
the world's want of a Saviour from sin as Isaiah
felt it. Never man saw so clearly that humanity is helpless and hopeless under the power
of evil unless God comes to the rescue. The
law's maker must be its keeper. He who
cursed sin must come and take it away. A
redeeming God, holy and therefore obedient,
loving and therefore suffering, faithful and
therefore triumphant,— this is the Immanuel
who is needed in a world of sin. Isaiah's soul
was driven by that need upward and upward
on the mount of vision, higher and higher in
the divine solitude of inspiration. From that
lofty height his voice floated down in songs of
glorious cheer to his fellow-men. "Comfort
ye, comfort ye, my people."[1] "Rejoice ye with
Jerusalem, and be glad with her, all ye that
love her: rejoice for joy with her, all ye that
mourn for her."[2]

But what was it that he saw to kindle that
singing hope in his soul? Nothing. He
dreamed, but there was really nothing for
him to see.

*The dream
departs.*
There was no roseate dawn on the far edge
of night, no auroral radiance of a virgin-born
Prince of Peace, no prophetic gleam of the

[1] Is. xl. 1.   [2] Is. lxvi. 10.

glory of a Kinsman Redeemer who should bear our griefs and carry our sorrows, who should be wounded for our transgressions, and by whose stripes we should be healed. When Isaiah thought that he saw the upward-breaking rays of such a brightness, it was but an illusion of sleep. There was no Christ. There was to be no Christ. God never intended it. Man only imagined it. The high and holy One who inhabiteth eternity looked upon the inhabitants of earth, "and he saw that there was no man, and wondered that there was no intercessor." [1] But His arm did not bring salvation unto Him, neither did His righteousness sustain Him. The Redeemer never meant to come to Zion. He was too great, too infinite to enter into human life, and be numbered with the transgressors, and bear the sin of many, and make intercession for the transgressors. The very thought of such an advent was folly and presumption.

Isaiah awakes from his dream. Every trace of the Christ disappears from his vision, blotted out in the encircling night. What is his message now? What song is left on his lips?

The prophet desolate.

A cry of woe and desolation. "They shall look unto the earth; and behold trouble and

[1] Is. lix. 16.

darkness, dimness of anguish ; and they shall be driven to darkness." [1] " Your iniquities have separated between you and your God, and your sins have hid his face from you, that he will not hear." [2]

The night descends.

There is no explanation of the mystery of evil. There is no light upon the future. There is only a shadow resting over all the earth, a shadow hiding the very face of God, — an unbroken shadow falling from the Old Testament without Christ.

[1] Is. viii. 22.   [2] Is. lix. 2.

II

The Intolerable Light

It may seem as if it were impossible to take *A book filled with Jesus.* Christ out of the New Testament without destroying it altogether. So entirely does the personality of Jesus pervade the book, that if He were withdrawn it would fall to pieces, like a tower from which the mortar had been all removed.

But it is not of Jesus as an example of noble *Jesus divided from Christ.* manhood, a teacher of moral truth, a worker of social reform, that I speak. It is of Jesus as the Christ, the divinely anointed redeemer of men, the bringer of salvation from sin. These two aspects of Jesus were, indeed, vitally united in fact. Yet it is possible to separate them in thought. It is conceivable that the New Testament might have reported Jesus to us as a prophet without making any revelation of Him as the Saviour.

Such a conception has already been entertained among men. It has been presented by some teachers, whose literary and historical sense is very imperfect, as an interpretation of what the New Testament actually is. It has been put forward by others, whose scholarship is better, as a theory of what the New Testament ought to be, and probably would have been, if it had been written in an age free from superstition.

A new kind of a New Testament. That which is really valuable in the book, we are told, is its picture of a beautiful character, its rules for good conduct, its spirit of piety and virtue, the clear light which it throws upon God and human life and immortality. If it contained only the Sermon on the Mount, it would still be complete and sufficient. The substance of it all could be put into an ethical creed. The essential Jesus is only the teacher and illustrator of a perfect morality. He is the central figure of Christianity not because He did more than man can do, but simply because He did what every man ought to do. All that goes beyond this in the New Testament, — all that refers to Him as the sacrifice for sin, the mediator between God and man, the only begotten Son who came forth from the bosom of the Father, was born and lived, was crucified and died, was buried and rose again, in order to redeem and reconcile the world to God, — is partly imaginary, and partly superstitious, and wholly unnecessary. A New Testament without Christ in this sense, would be not only possible, but very desirable.

The experiment may be tried. The testimony *What is it* of Jesus and the Apostles in regard to His work *worth?* as the Saviour may be obliterated, as the Russian censor "blacks out" the passages of a book which he deems dangerous. The cross as the central scene of the great reconciliation between man and God may be hidden. Christ as the deliverer from sin and death may be annulled in our thought. We shall then be able to estimate the meaning and value of the New Testament without Him.

There are two things in the book which must *Two points* strike every fair-minded reader. In two points *illuminated.* it is distinguished among all the books of the world. It gives a new and intensely searching view of the problem of moral evil. It is written from beginning to end in sight of death as the door which leads into eternity.

On these two points the New Testament pours an unrivalled light. Does it give us any comfort or hope in regard to them, without Christ?

It was Jesus of Nazareth who illuminated *What Jesus* the moral evil in the world most deeply and *says of sin.* clearly. He showed its spring, its secret workings, and the power which lies behind it. Calmly, steadily, with a sublime indifference to theory, with an inexorable sense of the facts of human life, He pressed His serene and faithful analysis of sin home to its centre in the inner life of man.

A falsehood on the lips means a lie in the heart. Violence in conduct means a cruel streak in character. Uncleanness in the life means impurity in the soul. "Those things which proceed out of the mouth come forth from the heart ; and they defile the man." [1]

The sanity of His doctrine. Jesus does not say that everything in human nature is evil. He does not say that all men are entirely depraved. He recognizes the good things that a good man bringeth forth out of his good treasure. [2] But he says also that all men, even the best, have need to be converted and become as little children ; [3] all men owe a vast debt which they are unable to pay ; [4] all men are unprofitable servants ; [5] all men have something to repent of, in the presence of God. [6]

The penetration of His doctrine. And this something which demands repentance is not outward and accidental ; it is inward and personal. It is the angry passion ; it is the impure imagination ; it is the secret unbelief which blinds the soul. All the excuses with which men cover and hide their sin grow

[1] Matt. xv. 18.
[2] Matt. xii. 35.
[3] Matt. xviii. 3.
[4] Matt. xviii. 23.
[5] Luke xvii. 10.
[6] Luke xiii. 3.

thin and transparent in the light of this searching analysis. Jesus reveals the underlying
facts. The sins of men are not the result of
circumstances, the fruit of outward tempta-
tions, things which belong to the world and
the age in which we live. They are things
which belong to us and come from us. The
fashions and forms of sin change with the centuries and differ in different lands. But the
essence of it is always the same. It comes
from within. The man in whose heart the root
is hidden is responsible for the fruit. This is
what Jesus says about the source of sin.

No less clear and penetrating is His teaching *The secret
in regard to its secret workings and its fatal *of the
heart.*
results. He reveals the truth that goodness
does not consist in obedience to the letter of
the law, but in harmony with its spirit. A
man may keep all the commandments, as the
young ruler did, and yet because he is selfish
he is outside of the kingdom of God.[1] A man
may observe all the Mosaic precepts and perform all the ritual of religion, as the Pharisee
did, and yet be a greater sinner than the Pub-
lican who stands afar off and beats upon his
breast.[2] Men are strangers to their own sins;

[1] Matt. xix.   [2] Luke xviii.

they do not recognize them when they meet them in the street. They are blind leaders of the blind, whose feet stumble in the gulf. The angry impulse is the "blot in the 'scutcheon." The real stain of blood is on the inside of the heart. The idle, irreverent word is blasphemy. There are no human lips that have not taken God's name in vain. The scorn of brethren is the little spark that kindles unquenchable flames. They in whose breast this spark smoulders are "in danger of hell-fire."[1] But they do not know it. They carry their lighted candles through the powder-magazine with their eyes shut.

The Sermon on the Mount. The Sermon on the Mount contains the most thorough diagnosis of sin that has ever been made. It proceeds by contrast with the symptoms of spiritual health and soundness. The Beatitudes are not only blessings to be desired; they are also tests to be applied to the heart. It was not without significance that this discourse was delivered from a lofty place. Its ideal of holiness rises as far above our actual life as an Alpine peak of stainless snow above the confusion and squalor and misery of the frail villages that hide in the valleys. "Be ye perfect even as your Father which is in heaven

[1] Matt. v. 22.

is perfect."[1] That summit is inaccessible if there is no divine Christ to lead and lift us thither.

But there is another element in the doctrine *The power behind sin.* of Jesus in regard to sin which we must not forget. He discloses a secret power behind it, which clothes it with strange terror and might. He teaches that there is a force, an influence, a spirit in the world, which is altogether evil, and which is continually desiring, seeking, and working sin. It is the unclean spirit rejoicing in the defilement of the house which it inhabits.[2] It is the father of lies ready to beget falsehood in every listening mind.[3] It is the enemy of souls sowing tares in the field by night.[4] It is Satan longing to get possession of the soul that he may sift it as wheat.[5]

Whether we take this teaching of Jesus lit- *The warning of Jesus.* erally or not, whether we believe that evil is embodied in demonic personality or not, one thing is unquestionable. Jesus regarded evil as a positive, organic, ever active, malignant power, a Prince of this world, whose domain lies all around us, whose influence touches us on every side, the friend of sin and the foe of the

[1] Matt. v. 48. [3] John viii. 44. [5] Luke xxii. 31.
[2] Matt. xii. 43 ff. [4] Matt. xiii. 39.

soul. There is a conflict going on in the world.
It is not a mere game.   It is an elemental war-
fare between right and wrong.   We are cast
into the midst of this conflict.   An unseen,
mighty, skilful, relentless adversary is against
us.   And in every heart there is a traitor ready
to betray the citadel into his hands.

The fear of Satan.   The additional fear which this mysterious
teaching of Jesus lends to the sense of sin made
itself felt in human experience for many centuries.   Doubtless it was over-emphasized and
exaggerated, by a false interpretation of His
words, into an immense and shapeless terror.
A grotesque and impossible devil tyrannized
over ages of superstition.   Men believed in a
Satan who was practically the rival of God,
equal in power if not in glory, and as immortal
in evil as God is in good.   There is no trace
of such a doctrine in the words of Jesus.[1]   It
was natural, it was inevitable, that men should
react from the exaggeration, and cast off almost
entirely, as they have done to-day, the thought
of an actual power of evil, outside of the human
soul and inexorably hostile to it.

But when we return to the teachings of
Jesus, and study them with candour and calm-
ness, we see that thought in His mind clearly

[1] *The Gospel for an Age of Doubt*, p. 272.

and unmistakably. He teaches us that our conflict is not merely with ourselves. There is an enemy against us who is mightier than man. We need a defender, a deliverer, a divine friend to fight with us and for us.

Where, then, shall we look for such a power- *Who will* ful friend? If Jesus was not the Christ who *fight for us?* came to save us from our sins, then there is no captain of salvation, no conqueror of Satan, no liberator of captive souls. We must fight the battle alone against unknown and heavy odds. The triumph of Jesus over evil was for Himself only. It gives no assurance that we also shall overcome the world. On the contrary, it makes our victory seem the more doubtful, when we remember His perfect courage and inflexible strength, in contrast with our waverings and the many defeats that we have already suffered. We have begun to lose the battle already. Who shall turn the tide for our discouraged forces?

The sinlessness of Jesus comforts us little *Jesus our* unless it has some remedial bearing upon our *example,* sins. If it is but an example of what every *only if He is our Saviour.* man ought to be, its very perfection daunts and disheartens us. Something less absolute and flawless would be better suited to our need.

In fact, men have never dared or cared to

make the stainless Jesus the real pattern of their lives, until they have learned to believe in Him as the redeeming sacrifice for their sins. They have chosen other ideals, other heroes, other examples, — less exacting, less disheartening, less depressing by contrast with themselves.

Has He no power to forgive?

It is the ransoming faith that " Christ suffered for us," that gives His disciples courage to say that He also left us "an example that we should follow in his steps."[1]   The idea of " The Imitation of Christ " is hopeful and inspiring only to the heart that has first felt the liberating touch of His pierced hand.   Sinners do not venture to go after the sinless Jesus unless they hear Him say " The Son of man hath power on earth to forgive sins."[2]

But in a Christless gospel this word has no place, no meaning.   There was no such unique power committed to the hands of Jesus.   All the consoling, reassuring, inspiriting utterances of Jesus, which are connected with His sublime confidence in His divine mission and authority to seek and save the lost, — utterances which strangely enough are closely and inseparably connected with the prevision of His death, His laying down His life for the sheep,[3] His lifting

[1] 1 Peter ii. 21.   [2] Matt. ix. 6.   [3] John x. 11.

up upon the cross,[1] — all these words of saving
hope must be "blacked out."

They lose their significance, if the Redeemer
is lost. There was no ransom wrought upon
the cross. There was only the payment of
the debt of nature. The good Shepherd
laid down His life. But it was not for the
sheep. It was only to show the cruelty of the
robbers. There was no victory on Calvary.
It was a defeat, in which the one sinless being
on earth was crushed and killed *by* the sin of
the world, — but not *for* it.

Let us turn from the Gospels to the Epistles, *The Epistles*
and consider what they have to say to us about *without*
Christ.
sin, when we have taken out of them the idea
of a work wrought by Jesus Christ for the
salvation of the world. It is evident that the
Apostles have received the teaching of their
Master in regard to the source, the workings,
the guilt, and the danger of sin, and that it has
made a profound impression upon them.

No doubt there was some difference between *St. Paul and*
St. John and St. Paul in regard to the philo- *St. John, —*
their teach-
sophic forms in which they expressed their *ing about*
thought upon this subject. St. Paul was trained *sin.*
in the rabbinical theology of Jerusalem. St.

[1] John iii. 14.

John was influenced by the Platonic philosophy
of Alexandria. St. Paul lays emphasis upon the
connection of sin with "the flesh," with man's
lower, physical nature.[1]   St. John brings out
"the darkness" of sin as contrasted with the
light of God.[2]   St. Paul traces the entrance of
sin into the world, to Adam's disobedience.[3]
St. John speaks of "the world" as an order of
existence estranged from God, which must not
be loved because it is opposed to the love of
God,[4] and declares that "the whole world lieth
in the Evil One."[5]   But both agree in teaching
that sin is transgression of the divine law;[6]
and that its fruit is death.[7]   It is their sense
of the reality and guilt of the transgression,
their overwhelming sense of the greatness of
the disaster which threatens all men on account
of it, that separates them as writers from the
easy-going, reckless pagan world.   "If we say
we have not sinned," says St. John, "we deceive
ourselves and the truth is not in us."[8]   "When
I would do good," cries St. Paul, "evil is

---

[1] Rom. vii. 5; viii. 4, 6; 2 Cor. x. 2; Gal. v. 17; Eph.
ii. 3.

[2] 1 John i. 6; ii. 9, 11; Rev. xvi. 10.

[3] Rom. v. 12-21.   [5] 1 John v. 19.

[4] 1 John ii. 15.   [6] 1 John iii. 4; Rom. vii. 13.

[7] Rom. vi. 23; viii. 6; 1 John iii. 14; v. 16; 2 Cor.
xv. 56.   [8] 1 John i. 8.

present with me. O wretched man that I am, who shall deliver me from the body of this death?"[1]

But if this is all that they have to say to us, *Is this all?* if they bring us no message of a divine Christ who hath appeared to put away sin, how lame and impotent is their conclusion! Read St. Paul's answer to his own question, who is to deliver him, with Christ left out: 'I thank God, *through nobody*.' Read St. John's consolation to those who have sinned, without the gospel of atonement. 'If any man sin, we have no advocate with the Father, neither is there any propitiation for our sins, nor for the sins of the whole world.' 'Herein is love, not that we loved God, but that he did not love us, neither did send his Son to be the justification for our sins.'

Go on a little further with this Christless *A negative gospel?* New Testament. Listen to St. Paul again: 'For as through one man sin entered into the world, and death through sin, and so death passed unto all men, for that all sinned,— even so there was no grace of God, and the gift of grace by the one man, Jesus Christ, did not abound unto many.' 'Sin reigned unto death, but grace did not reign through righteousness

[1] Rom. vii. 21, 24.

unto eternal life through Jesus Christ our
Lord.' 'God commendeth his love towards us
in that while we were yet sinners nobody died
for us.' 'Wherefore remember that ye were
aliens from the commonwealth of Israel and
strangers to the covenants of promise; and
now ye that were far off are not made nigh by
the blood of Christ.' 'God is not in Christ
reconciling the world unto himself.' 'There is
no mediator between God and man.' 'The
life that I now live in the flesh I live by faith
in myself, for the Son of God did not love me,
nor give himself for me.'

Listen to the author of the Epistle to the
Hebrews: 'Having then no high priest who
hath passed into the heavens, let us not draw
near with boldness unto the throne of grace,
for we have no promise of mercy, nor grace to
help in time of need.' 'For we are not come
unto Jesus the mediator of the new covenant,
and to the blood of sprinkling which speaketh
better things than that of Abel, but unto Mt.
Sinai that burns with fire.'

Listen to St. Peter: 'We know that we
were not redeemed, neither with corruptible
things as silver and gold, nor with the precious
blood of Christ as of a lamb without blemish
and without spot.' 'Wherefore, not having

seen him, we love him not, neither do we rejoice in him, since we receive not the end of
our faith, nor the salvation of our souls.'

This is what the New Testament would say
to a world of sin, without Christ. It is surely
not consoling.

But the significance of this teaching is very *Death and*
much intensified and deepened by the view *the future.*
which the New Testament gives of death as the
gateway of another life.

The heathen world in the first century was
for the most part inclined to cover up the fact
of death as much as possible, to hide it in
flowers, to put it out of sight. But the Christians, perhaps because they were persecuted and
afflicted and continually in danger of death,
perhaps because they had a truer and a braver
philosophy of life, followed another course.
They faced death steadily, looked it in the
eyes, prepared to meet it, and conquered all its
terrors by their faith in Christ as the Saviour.

There is no other book in the world which
can compare with the New Testament in its
serene, unflinching recognition of death's in-
evitableness. There is no other book in the
world which has so clear and courageous an
insight into its eternal issues. From beginning

a

to end it is pervaded with the conviction that
" It is appointed unto all men once to die, and
after death the judgment."

The burden of death.   Now the burden of death is twofold.   There
is a burden of present sorrow and anguish, in
the sufferings of the flesh which precede and
accompany it, and in the pains of the spirit
which are associated with the breaking of human ties and the bereavement of love.   There
is also a burden of fear and anxiety for the
future, a sense of apprehension in regard to the
perils and mysteries of the unknown world.

The faith that lightens it.   Both of these burdens, in the New Testament,
are lifted and bravely borne by trust in Christ.
It is the sense of fellowship with Him in their
sufferings that sustains the Christians in the
valley of the shadow of death.   It is the confidence that He has risen from the dead and that
He will plead for them at the judgment, that
enables them to face the future with composure.
But if Christ is taken away, both burdens fall
back with new and crushing weight upon the
heart.   " If Christ be not risen, then is our
preaching vain, and your faith is also vain."
"If in this life only we have hope in Christ,
we are of all men most miserable." [1]

What practical assurance, what tangible

[1] Cor. xv. 14, 19.

proof, is there of a divine sympathy in our
sufferings, without the vision of the Son of God
who has borne our griefs and carried our sorrows? The God of nature, the God who made
the heavens bright and beautiful with stars, and
ordained the immutable glories of the revolving
year, — what can He understand of the pains
that rack our human hearts, what part has He
in the broken and tragical drama of mortal life?
A sublime spectator,

"He sees with equal eyes, as God of all,
A hero perish or a sparrow fall."

I think a man or woman with a breaking
heart, pierced with the spear of pain, smitten
with the anguish of inexorable separation,
might go out into this splendid world in
the spring, when the glory of earth's face is
renewed with joy and the time for the singing
of birds is come, — such a lonely, desolate, per-
ishing man or woman might walk among the
unconscious flowers, and look up to the silent-
shining sky, and the unfriended heart would
break again with the thought that there is after
all no clear word of divine sympathy with it, —
no human life of God, no Christ who wept at
the grave of Lazarus, and agonized in the garden, and died on the cross, in order that He

How do we know of God's sympathy?

Nature's indifference.

might know, with us, the mortal sorrows of a world of sin and death.

The risen Christ. What comfort, what peace, is there in the New Testament view of death, unless we can see beyond it what St. Paul saw when he said, "I know whom I have believed, and am persuaded that he is able to keep that which I have committed unto him against that day."[1] — "O death, where is thy sting? O grave, where is thy victory? The sting of death is sin; and the strength of sin is the law. But thanks be to God, which giveth us the victory through our Lord Jesus Christ."[2] Annul that gospel of victory over death by One who has taken away the sting of sin, and what remains? A certain fearful looking-for of judgment; a long vision of futurity with no reasonable hope of escape from evil and its consequences; a prospect of dying without getting rid of the disease which kills us.

"Now He is dead." Read again the words of the Apostles after you have blotted out their gospel of the conquest of death by Christ. 'Through death he was destroyed by him that had the power of death, that is, the devil, and brought no deliverance to them who through fear of death were all their lifetime subject to bondage.'

[1] 2 Tim. i. 12.   [2] 1 Cor. xv. 55–57.

'God hath not raised him up, neither were the pains of death loosed, because it was not possible that he should escape from it.' 'The enemy that shall never be destroyed is death.' 'This same Jesus shall never come again.' 'He liveth not to make intercession for his people.' 'Even as he never was offered to bear the sin of many, so shall he never again appear without sin unto salvation to them that wait for him.' 'If we believe not that Jesus died and rose again, even so them also which sleep with Jesus will God never bring with him.'

> "Christ is not risen!
> Eat, drink, and die, for we are souls bereaved;
> Of all the creatures under heaven's high cope,
> We are most hopeless, who once had most hope,
> And most beliefless, that had most believed.
> Ashes to ashes, dust to dust,
> As of the unjust, also of the just;
> Yea, of that Just One too,
> It is the one sad Gospel that is true, —
> Christ is not risen!"[1]

To take Christ out of the Bible is to make it worse than useless to a sinful world. It is to make it crushing, disheartening, terrifying, — the saddest book that was ever written. The Old Testament casts upon us an unbroken

The Book that bans.

---

[1] A. H. Clough, *Easter Day, 1849.*

shadow of gloomy fate.   The New Testament pierces it with an intolerable light of conscious guilt and coming judgment.

The restoration of Christ.   But restore Christ to His place in the Bible, and it becomes the book of hope and joy.   The unbroken shadow is changed into the adumbration of the coming Redeemer : the shadow Christ [1] whose angel moves before the struggling host of all who will follow God's guidance through the wilderness of sin.   The intolerable light is transformed into a blessed healing radiance : the light of the knowledge of the glory of God in the face of Jesus Christ, the Saviour of the world.

[1] *The Shadow Christ, an introduction to Christ Himself.* By Gerald Stanley Lee.   The Century Company.

IV

CHRIST'S MISSION TO THE INNER LIFE

What, then, is the service rendered to the world by Christianity? The proclamation of "good news." And what is this good news? The pardon of sin. The God of holiness loving the world and reconciling it to Himself by Jesus, in order to establish the Kingdom of God, the city of souls, the life of heaven upon earth, — here you have the whole of it; but in this is a revolution.

— AMIEL's *Journal*, Jan. 27, 1869.

IV

CHRIST'S MISSION TO THE INNER LIFE

THE ultimate mission of Christ was to the *A pro-* inner life of man. *gramme in outline.*

His ministry there was not in words alone, but in character and action ; in what He was and what He did for men ; the heart of His message was Himself, His life, His death.

The central gospel of this message is the reality and completeness of peace with God through the forgiveness of sins.

The forgiveness of sins brings with it the freedom and power of a new inner life of divine righteousness.

These four statements may serve to mark out, in a broad way, the line of thought that I wish to follow in this chapter.

I

The Kingdom is within You

The seat of empire.   Christ came into the world to proclaim and establish the kingdom of God among men. The sway of that kingdom extends over every region of our life.   But its seat must be within us.

It must reach and reconcile and rule that interior region of the heart which lies behind audible utterance and visible action, below social ties and bonds of human fellowship, underneath conscious reasonings and formulated theories, — that undiscovered country where the moral sentiments, the religious feeling, the sense of dependence, and the joy or grief of living, have their home.

The springs of life.   It is there that the real forces of human life are generated.   Man is the one creature in the universe in whom the mechanical counts least, and the spiritual counts most.   Not only his personal happiness, but also his actual power and efficiency in the world depend upon the condition of his inner life.   He could not "live by bread alone," even if he would.   Every phase of his existence betrays the presence of an energy, whether for good or for evil, which is drawn from some secret source deep within him, and fed by streams which flow far below the surface of his physical nature.

Vitality, in man, is a spiritual force conditioned, but not created, by a material embodiment. A *vitometer* will never be invented, because there is no instrument delicate enough to take the temperature of the inner life. Even in dealing with bodily disease, the wise physician, while he may make his diagnosis absolute, always recognizes an element of uncertainty in his prognosis. "While there is life there is hope," he says. He might add, "While there is hope there is life." Hope has healed more diseases than any medicine.

The life of man is a demonstrated daily miracle. It shows that the physical laws which we know and the physical forces which we can measure, are traversed by spiritual laws which we do not know and spiritual forces which we cannot measure. It proves the reality and potency of that which is invisible and imponderable.

The various kinds of energy which are developed from heat are not more real, nor more powerful, than the actual working force which is developed in the world from love in the inner life of man. Gravitation itself does no *Spiritual forces.*

more to insure the stability of the material order, than inward peace of soul does to maintain the stability of the social order. The wind that bloweth where it listeth, is no more efficient in purifying and vitalizing the atmosphere, than are the secret spiritual currents of penitence and faith and aspiration which breathe through the hearts of men, in cleansing and renewing the inner air which keeps the soul alive.

Sin deadens all. This is the reason why sin is a power of disorder and death. It is not because it affects the outer life, not because it sows the seeds of physical corruption and decay, not because it brings forth crimes of violence and destruction. It is because it pervades the inner life, because it poisons the streams of human existence at the fountain-head, because it paralyzes the vital energies of humanity.

Sin is a separating, secluding, imprisoning power which shuts the soul off from the purifying breath of the divine Spirit and leaves it in a dungeon, to breathe the same air over and over again until it is smothered. Sin is a rebellious, turbulent, tormenting power which destroys the inward peace of the soul, agitates it with restless passion, tortures it with haunting fear. Sin is a selfish, envious, hateful power which takes the very life out of love and makes it impotent for good, a vain dream never to be realized, a beautiful, ineffectual ghost.

The supreme directness, the triumphant sim- *Jesus knew* plicity of Jesus as the restorer of humanity to *the seat of disorder.* its true order and the bringer of a new kingdom into the world, came from the clearness with which He saw that the world's chief trouble and man's deepest need lie in the inner life. He wasted no strength in polishing the outside of the cups and platters on which man's exterior wants are served. He spent no time in whitening sepulchres. He knew that the seat of real goodness and permanent happiness and divine harmony must be in the inner life. The incomparable service to mankind which was to give Him the eternal chieftaincy in the spiritual life, was a service to the soul.

There can be no real empire of peace unless *He sought* this deepest region is reached. There must be *the centre.* no nook or corner or crevice of man's life left unexplored, unsubdued, unreconciled ; no lurking-place of rebellion ; no fountain of discord ; no

> "little rift within the lute,
> That by and by will make the music mute,
> And ever widening slowly silence all."

The kingdom must go in to the centre and down to the bottom of personality, and work from within outward, — from below upward. This was the programme of Christ; and to carry it out He directed His journey to the inner life of man.

Blessings by the way. On the way thither, like a prince in progress, He conferred inestimable gifts and blessings in the outer circles of human existence. The doctrine of Jesus has widened the thoughts of men. The example of Jesus has crystallized the moral aspirations of men into a flawless and imperishable ideal. The precept of Jesus has struck the keynote for a new harmony of human fellowship. The influence of Jesus has given inspiration and guidance to philosophy and literature and the fine arts.

The inward quest. But as we follow Him through these regions we are made aware that He is pressing inward to a goal beyond. He seeks the thinker, we say, behind the thought; the person, behind the social order. He aims to elevate man by uplifting men. His mission is not to masses, nor to classes; it is to the individual. But when He finds the individual, as a thinker, as a social unit, what then? Still Christ seems to press inward, to seek a yet deeper point.

His mission to society is through the indi-

vidual.   But when we have said that, we have
not yet said all.   His mission to the individual
is through the inner life.   He has not arrived
at the goal of His journey, He has not spoken
the last word of His message until He has said
to the paralytic, "Son, be of good cheer, thy
sins are forgiven thee"; and to the woman of
Syro-Phœnicia, "Go in peace"; and to the
disciples, "Let not your heart be troubled";
and to all the weary and heavy-laden, "Come
unto me, and ye shall find rest unto your
souls."

The kingdom of God which Jesus proclaims *A kingdom*
and establishes is a kingdom of the soul.   Its *of the soul.*
deepest meaning is a personal experience.   Its
essence is righteousness and peace and joy in
the Holy Ghost.   Its dwelling-place and seat
of power is in the inner life.

II

The Picture of Jesus in the Soul

The imprint of Christ.   If this be true, it is perfectly natural, and altogether reasonable, that the earliest and clearest and most enduring manifestation of Christ should be in this region of man's inmost being. The impress of His character should be deepest upon the sub-liminal self. The traces of His presence in the world should be most distinct and most indelible in the records of spiritual experience. The evidences of His healing, purifying, harmonizing, saving power should be found first and most abundantly in those underlying relations, those mysterious sentiments and propensities, —

> "those obstinate questionings
> Of sense and outward things,
> Fallings from us, vanishings;
> *Blank misgivings of a creature*
> *Moving about in worlds not realized,*
> *High instincts before which our mortal Nature*
> *Doth tremble like a guilty thing surprised:*
> Those first affections,
> Those shadowy recollections,
> Which, be they what they may,
> Are yet the fountain light of all our day."

And so in fact we find it to be. The image of Jesus comes to light, first of all, in the

spiritual experience of man. The earliest and
the most wonderful picture of Him is simply a
living reflection of Him in man's inner life.

Before we can discern any influence of His   *As many*
teaching, as a great reformer, upon the institu-   *as received*
    Him.
tions of society; before we can perceive any
effect of those large, simple truths which He
brought to light, upon the orderly thinking of
the world; before we can trace the rudest
beginnings of Christian art, the most ancient
formulas of Christian worship, the earliest foun-
dations of Christian temples; yes, even before
we can find any narrative of the life of Jesus,
any collection of His sayings, any record of
His deeds,— first of all, and most vivid of all,
we see the person of Jesus printed upon the
hearts and revealed in the letters of certain men
who loved and trusted and adored Him as their
Saviour from sin.

As a matter of fact, the Epistles come before   *The Epistles*
the Gospels. I do not say they are any more   *antedate the*
    Gospels.
authentic, any more precious, than the Gospels.
I do not say they are ever to be read or interpreted apart from the Gospels. But I say they
are forever sacred and authoritative to all Christian hearts, because they are the place where we
first catch sight of Jesus Christ in this world.
And their personal testimony, their peculiar sig-

H

nificance, their religious meaning, must never
be forgotten or denied, if we want to know
what Christ came to do, and what Christ really
did, for the life of man.

For what are these Epistles? They are not
formal treatises of theology, of ethics, of church
government. They are simply transcripts of
the spiritual experience of real men, — St. Peter
and St. Paul and St. John, and perhaps some
others whose names we do not know.

Christ their theme. No one can doubt that the centre of these
letters is Jesus Christ. He is their theme and
their inspiration, their impulse and their aim.
They are written in His name. They bear witness to His power, they glow with His praise.
They are, first of all, and most of all, evidences
of the place which Jesus held in the inner life
of these men, testimonies to the change which
He wrought in their souls, — a change so great,
so deep, so joyful, that it was like a new birth,
a veritable passing from death unto life. Listen
to a description of this change, in words as fresh
and glowing as if they had been written but
yesterday: —

*Their wit-
ness to His
power.* "Therefore if any man be in Christ, he is
a new creature : old things are passed away ;
behold, all things are become new. And all
things are of God, who hath reconciled us to

himself by Jesus Christ, and hath given to us
the ministry of reconciliation; to wit, that
God was in Christ, reconciling the world unto
himself, not imputing their trespasses unto
them; and hath committed unto us the word
of reconciliation. Now then we are ambassadors for Christ, as though God did beseech
you by us : we pray you in Christ's stead, be
ye reconciled to God. For he hath made him to
be sin for us, who knew no sin ; that we might
be made the righteousness of God in him."

This is an authentic description of the mission of Christ to the inner life of man. This is
a reflection of what He really effected in the
secret place of the human heart. This is the
voice of that new tide of peace which silently
rose through man's experience, —

The original gospel.

> "One common wave of thought and joy
> Lifting mankind again."

This is the original gospel, which began to win
the world eighteen hundred years ago, and has
never ceased to spread from heart to heart,
from land to land, like music mixed with light.

And it is the faithful and persistent witness
to this experience, more than anything else,
that has made Christianity a world-religion.
A changed heart, uttering its new-found fe-

licity in sweet and searching tones, — this is
the miracle that has drawn the attention of
men, century after century, to the teachings
of Christianity.

*A joyful
change.*
Its apostles won their way chiefly by the
evidence which they gave that something had
happened within them to transform their life
at the fountain-head.   The sense of newness
in their souls was the source of their power.
Whenever this sense of newness has faded and
grown dim, the self-propagating force of Christianity has waned.   Whenever this sense of
newness has been deep and vivid, Christianity
has advanced swiftly and found a wide welcome.   Its most potent argument has been this
simple and direct testimony to the pacification
and renewal of the inner life by the accept-
ance of Jesus Christ as the Saviour.

*What did it
mean?*
I am not concerned at present to justify it,
to defend it, to argue for its truth or its morality, to find a place for it in a system of
theology or philosophy.   What I want to do
is just to tell what it was; to show what it
meant to the men who received it; to look at
it, not as a theory, not as a doctrine, but as a
spiritual experience; to let the inner life speak
for itself about what Christ has done for the
souls of those who have believed on Him.

III

Peace with God through Christ

That Christ's mission was one of joy and peace needs no proof. The New Testament is a book that throbs and glows with inexpressible gladness. It is the one bright spot in the literature of the first century. The Christians were the happiest people in the world. Poor, they were rich; persecuted, they were exultant; martyred, they were victorious. The secret of Jesus, as they knew it, was a blessed secret. It filled them with the joy of living. Their watchword was, " Rejoice and be exceeding glad." *The gladness of Christianity*

But what were the elements of that joy? What was it that had entered into their inner life thus to transform and illuminate it?

To answer this question fully would be to give a summary of the primitive records of Christianity. All the manifold aspects of human existence were affected, unmistakably and immediately, by faith in Jesus Christ as the Son of God and the Saviour of men. Those who received Him thus into their hearts felt that they were saved. And if one had asked them from what they were saved, doubtless *Salvation.*

they would have wondered at the question, and would have answered, "From everything that brings trouble and fear and anguish and death into our souls."

All things made new. The world looked to them like a new place, and they felt like new men. Sorrow was changed. Instead of a hopeless burden of affliction, it had become the means of working out for them a far more exceeding and eternal weight of glory. Death was changed. Instead of a gloomy shadow enveloping the end of all things, it had become the gateway into a world of light. Duty was changed. Instead of an impossible compliance with an inexorable law, it had become a new obedience with divine help to accomplish it. They felt that they had received power in the inner life to become the sons of God. And the chief element in this power, according to their own testimony, was the sense of deliverance from the weight, the curse, the condemnation of their sins, through the work of the Lord Jesus Christ.

It is of this strange and wonderful feeling of salvation from sin that I wish to speak more particularly, not as a doctrine, not as a theory, but as an actual fact brought by Christ into the inner life of man.

1. The normal Christian experience, as it *Sin taken* is expressed by those who stand nearest to *away.* Christ, utters itself, first of all, as a great sense of peace with God through something which Christ has done to sweep away the barrier of sin between the human and the divine.

Nowhere else in the world do we find such a deep and keen sense of sin, and of its three deadly facts, as Henry Drummond calls them, — its power, its stain, and its guilt; nowhere else in the world do we find these facts so clearly recognized, so profoundly felt, as in the New Testament.

In many of our modern religious writers this sense of sin seems to be a vanishing quantity. Mr. Gladstone says: "They appear to have a very low estimate both of the quantity and the quality of sin; of its amount, spread like a deluge over the world, and of the subtlety, intensity, and virulence of its nature."[1] It is chiefly in the secular writers, the dramatists like Ibsen, the novelists like Hardy, that we find a full and clear recognition of the facts of moral evil to-day. And they offer no remedy, give no hope.

But when we turn back to the New Testa-

[1] W. E. Gladstone, *Later Gleanings*, p. 114.

ment we come into touch with men who faced the facts, and, at the same time, felt that they had found the cure.

Nothing that Jesus said or did, led His disciples to minimize or disregard sin, to cover it up with flowers, to transform it into a mere defect or mistake, to deny its reality and explain it away, to say

"The evil is naught, is null, is silence implying sound."

The whole effect of His mission, whatever form it may have taken, whatever its teaching may have been, — its undeniable effect was to intensify and deepen the consciousness of sin as a fatal thing from which men must needs be saved.

"This is the condemnation," says St. John, "that light is come into the world, and men loved darkness rather than light, because their deeds were evil."[1] "All have sinned and come short of the glory of God," says St. Paul; "death passed upon all men, for that all have sinned."[2] "For whosoever shall keep the whole law," says St. James, "and yet offend in one point, he is guilty of all."[3] "If we say we have not sinned," says St. John, "we make God a liar and his truth is not in us."[4]

[1] John iii. 19.
[2] Rom. v. 12.
[3] James ii. 10.
[4] 1 John i. 10.

But with this overwhelming sense of sin *The perfect release.* which Christ brought into the inner life, He brought also an equally great and deep sense of deliverance from it.

"There is therefore now no condemnation to them that are in Christ Jesus, who walk not after the flesh but after the Spirit." [1] "And you, being dead in your sins, hath he quickened together with him, having forgiven you all trespasses." [2] If any man "have committed sins, they shall be forgiven unto him." [3] "I write unto you, little children, because your sins are forgiven you for his name's sake." [4]

Now it is an extraordinary thing that men should speak thus, in one breath condemning themselves and in the next breath declaring their freedom from condemnation. And when we come to look into this strange utterance of the inner life, we find that it flows from a twofold experience.

2. First of all, there is a profound, unalter- *The certainty of God's love.* able conviction that the life and death of Jesus Christ are an expression of the forgiving love of God toward man. The old idea of God as a stern, angry, revengeful being, demand-

---

[1] Rom. viii. 1.   [3] James v. 15.
[2] Col. ii. 13.   [4] 1 John ii. 12.

ing and delighting in the death of the sinner, has vanished from the inner life of the true Christian. Somehow Christ has blotted it out. Somehow the Christian knows that God is love. And if we ask how he knows it, the answer is, that the only begotten Son came forth from the bosom of the Father to reveal Him. "Herein is love, not that we loved God, but that he loved us, and sent his Son to be the propitiation for our sins." [1] "God commendeth his love toward us, in that while we were yet sinners, Christ died for us." [2] All the meaning of Christ's life and death, with us and for us, hangs upon His being the true Son of God, the word of God, the brightness of the Father's glory and the express image of His person. [3] It is this that makes us sure that God is not a fierce, vindictive, relentless God. He is more than a ruler, a judge of all the earth, an almighty king. He is our friend, the lover of our souls. He is willing to live among us, to suffer with us, to die for us.

Christ one with the Father. The entire significance of Christ as a revelation of divine Love depends upon His real oneness with the Father, and the essential voluntariness of His sacrifice. It is not a punish-

[1] 1 John iv. 10.　　　[2] Rom. v. 8.
[3] *Gospel for an Age of Doubt*, pp. 105, 120.

ment inflicted from without, by the inexorable law of God. It is a revelation made from within, by the immeasurable love of God, showing mercy at the heart of righteousness.

The faith in Christ's divinity underlies the faith in His sacrifice as an expression of the kindness of God's heart. It could not speak to us of the love of God unless the love of God were in it. Love is the light within the lantern. There would be no colour in the glass, the figure of the crucifix would be black and indistinguishable, if it were not transfigured by that inner radiance.

The love of God goes before the gift of Christ. "God so loved the world that he gave his only begotten Son." He did not give His only begotten Son in order that He might learn to love the world. *Love the precedent.*

The love was expressed not only in the life, it was summed up and crowned in the death, of Christ. "Greater love hath no man than this, that a man lay down his life for his friends." Greater love hath no god than this. Love's consummation is the cross.

It is not intended to produce a change in the mind of God. It is intended to show what is already in the mind of God. It is not designed to make Him feel differently toward

men. It is designed to reveal what He has
always felt. It is not love's manufacture. It
is love's disclosure.

Forgiveness and repentance. Men say that repentance is the condition of
forgiveness. Only let a man repent of his sin,
only let him be sorry for it, and hate it, and
turn to God, crying for pardon, and he shall be
forgiven. This is a glorious, an inspiring view
of the readiness of divine mercy.

But the picture of Jesus in the soul, as it is
drawn in the New Testament, goes far beyond
the glory of this thought. It shows us that
in Christ forgiveness is the creator of repentance. God is ready to forgive long before man
is ready to repent. God gives His Son to die
for us while we are yet sinners. At the heart
of the gift lies the desire to make us sorry for
our sins. "The goodness of God leadeth thee
to repentance."[1] To forgive is divine; that
comes first. To repent is human; that follows
afterward.

Christ did not make God love the world. In all the New Testament I can find no trace
of the idea that Christ did anything, or needed
to do anything, to make God love the world.

There is a noble passage in the works of
St. Augustine, which sets forth the true image
of Christ as the expression of God's readiness

[1] Rom. ii. 4.

to forgive sins. "What is meant," he asks, "by 'being reconciled by the death of his Son'? Was it, indeed, so that when God the Father was angry with us He saw the death of His Son, and was appeased? Was, then, the Son already so appeased toward us that He was willing to die for us; while the Father was so angry that unless the Son had died He would not have been appeased? What does it mean, then, when the same teacher of the Gentiles says, in another place, 'What shall we say to these things? If God be for us, who can be against us? He that spared not his own Son but freely delivered him up for us all, how has he not with him also freely given us all things?' Unless the Father had been already appeased, would He have delivered up His own Son, not sparing Him for us? Is there not a contradiction between these two views? In the former the Son dies for us, and the Father is reconciled by His death. In the latter the Father, as if out of love for us, does not spare the Son, but Himself, for our sake, delivers Him up to death. But I see that the Father loved us beforehand, — not only before the Son died, but also before the world was created, according to the testimony of the Apostle who says, 'He hath chosen us in him before **the** foundation of the world.' Nor was the Son unwillingly offered, for it is said of Him, 'Who loved me, and gave himself for me.' Therefore together, both the Father and the Son, and the Spirit of both, work all things at the same time equally and harmoniously; yet we are justified in the blood of Christ, and we are reconciled to God by the death of His Son." [1]

So stands the picture of Christ the mediator, the reconciler, as it is reflected in the soul of those who first trusted in Him.

God's love antedates atonement.   His atonement does not reconcile God to the world. No need of that. God has loved the world forever.

It does reconcile the world to God. Great need of that. For it breaks down the barrier of fear and mistrust; it rends the veil of dreadful dreams that sin has woven before the divine face, and discloses the countenance of a pitying, forgiving Father; it moves men to repentance by the mightiest force of mercy; it binds men to holy living by the enduring bonds of gratitude and love.

The necessity of sacrifice.   3. But could the sacrifice of Christ have meant this much to the inner life of man unless it had also meant something more? Suppose for a moment that the disciples had thought that it

[1] Augustine, *De Trinitate*, Book XIII. ch. xi.

was not really a necessary sacrifice; that there
was no reason why He should suffer, except
perhaps that His sufferings might move their
hearts; that His death was nothing more than
the accidental consequence of His being entan-
gled in a world like this; that God could have
forgiven sin and would have forgiven sin in just
the same way if there had been no crucifixion
on Calvary. What then? Would Christ still
have had the same atoning power to draw their
hearts to God?

It is love that reconciles. And it is self- *Love always*
sacrifice that reveals love. But does an un- *serviceable.*
necessary sacrifice, a useless sacrifice, reveal love
in a way that moves and compels our hearts?

No, the moment we perceive that an offered
proof of love has no relation to our real needs,
and is not intended to do us any real good, it
loses its power upon us, becomes unreal and
futile. Suppose, for example, that you are
rowing a boat on a river, in no danger of any
kind. A friend comes down to the shore and
hails you; he tells you that he is about to
show his devotion to you in a way that you
cannot possibly doubt. He intends to give
his life for you. So he throws himself into
the water and is drowned. Are you impressed
with gratitude and love? Is the proof of de-

votion so manifest and indubitable that you
cannot resist it? Does it not seem more like
a vain show of heroism, a display made not so
much for your sake as for the sake of him who
made it?

But if your boat had been sinking? Ah,
then it would have been another matter.
The man who gives up his life to rescue you
from an actual peril, commands your love because he is your saviour. The crown of love is
service. The glory of sacrifice is usefulness.
The love of Christ, the sacrifice of Christ, draw
their deepest power upon the inner life of man
from the conviction they really have accomplished a deliverance for sinners from the guilt
and curse and doom of sin.

*The inter-
pretation of
the Cross.*
The first message that the disciples received
from the risen Jesus, while their minds were
still overwhelmed by the apparent tragedy of
the crucifixion, was the truth that it was not a
useless loss, but a fruitful gain. The subject
of His conversation with the two sad-hearted
Christians on the road to Emmaus, — sad because they could not see why it was necessary
for Christ to die, — the theme of His talk with
them was the need of His death. "Ought not
Christ to have suffered these things and to
have entered into His glory?"

How much the first Apostles, who had been *The tragedy on Calvary.* with Jesus from the beginning, who had loved Him and trusted that He was the promised Redeemer of Israel, — how much these men needed this gospel of a real victory in **His** death, we who have always heard it, even though we may not have believed in it, can hardly realize. Think what it must have meant to see the holy and loving Master die upon the cross. What a crushing catastrophe, what an inexplicable tragedy, what an irreparable loss for the world! How was it possible to have any trust in the wisdom and goodness of a God who would permit such a cruel disaster? How was it possible to have any hope for a humanity which had no other use for the perfect life than to blot it out in anguish and disgrace? Faith itself must have died with Christ, unless it had been able to discover a meaning, a purpose, a necessity, a triumph in His death great enough to make it the accomplishment of all that He had lived for. A bitter waste, or an unspeakable gain : those were the alternatives in the cross.

One would think that the words of Jesus *Christ's prevision of victorious death.* while He was with the disciples had been clear enough to show them which was the true explanation. He had spoken of His death as inevitable; He had moved forward to it as the fulfilment of His mission; He had interpreted it as an infinite benefit to His disciples. "The Son of man came to give his life a ransom for many." "The bread that I will give is my flesh, which I will give for the life of the world." "Except a corn of wheat fall into the ground and die, it abideth alone; but if it die, it bringeth forth much fruit." "I, if I be lifted up, will draw all men unto me." "This cup is the New Covenant in my blood which is shed for many for the remission of sins."

The doubts of the disciples.

But the meaning of these words was withheld from their eyes. They did not dare, they were not willing, to look the fact of Christ's coming death in the face, as He did. So its significance escaped them. It needed the lifting up of the cross, it needed the vision of the Master's death, to make them realize the true alternative.

The alternative.

On Calvary all was lost, — unless, on Calvary all was won! The disciples stood between utter despair and immeasurable hope. The risen Lord came back to tell them that all was won by the needful sacrifice of the cross. That is the testimony of the first Apostles.

Paul's testimony comes out of a different experience but leads to the same result. He had been an unbeliever in Jesus, a hater and

a persecutor of the Nazarene.   To him the man *Paul's*
of Nazareth had appeared as a false prophet, *experience.*
a blasphemer.   He found no fault with the
death of Jesus from that point of view.   It
was not only necessary; it was desirable.
Paul would have willingly consented to it, if
he had been in the palace of Caiaphas, and
in the judgment-hall of Pilate, and on the
hill called Golgotha.

But when Paul was overwhelmingly convinced that he was wrong in his judgment of
the Nazarene, his old point of view was utterly
destroyed.

From the eternal moment on the Damascus *The changed*
road when Paul saw that the crucified Jesus *point of*
view.
whom he had been persecuting was not a here-
tic Jew, justly slain for his blasphemies, but
the true and living Christ of God, — from that
moment it became absolutely necessary for him
to find a new interpretation of the cross.   He
never dreamed that it could be regarded as
a mere incident, a needless sacrifice, a dis-
astrous close of a beautiful life.   It must be
an essential element, an indispensable factor
in the mission of the Messiah.   It must complete the revelation of God which was made
in Him.   It must be the corner-stone of that
divine kingdom which He came to establish.

The start-ing-point of his theology.

This was the starting-point of Paul's theology. While he thought that Jesus was not the Christ, he saw in the death on the cross nothing but the punishment of the folly and falsehood of the Nazarene. As soon as he was convinced that Jesus really was the Christ, the death on the cross was transformed into the revelation of the righteousness and love of God. There was no other alternative. The sinless one, the glorious one, did not die for sins of His own. He could not have died in vain. Therefore He must have died for us. God was manifest in Him reconciling the world unto Himself.

The Chris-tian view of the cross.

This was certainly the interpretation which the Christians put upon the death of their holy Lord and Master on the cross. This was the effect that it actually wrought in their inner life. They did not deem it an accident, nor a catastrophe. It was not the defeat, nor merely the termination, of His work. It was the crown and consummation of His work. It gave Christ to them more than it took Him from them. They did not think that He died for naught. His death for sinners was the greatest service that love could perform. It accomplished and declared God's righteousness in the remission of sins that are past. It made

it possible for God to be just and the justifier
of him which believeth in Jesus.

The Apostles did not teach that forgiveness
could not have taken place without the crucifixion of Christ. They kept within the horizon
of experience. They testified of what they
knew, and bore witness of what they had seen.

They simply taught that, without the death *The effect
of Christ, forgiveness would not have been *of Christ's
death.*
what it is. They taught it because they felt
it. They did not dream that the tragedy of
the cross made any change in God. But they
were sure that it made a change in the relation
of the sinful world to God. It took away the
curse of the law. It blotted out the hand-
writing of ordinances. It redeemed us. It
brought us near to God. It put away sin. It
cleansed us from sin in the blood of Christ.
It is the one offering by which Christ hath
perfected them that are sanctified.

Now, what were the secret laws and what *The hidden
were the mysterious relations of the world to *relations.*
God which made this offering of the sinless life
of Jesus necessary for the rescue of mankind
from sin, no man knoweth, nor can any man
explain them and set them in order. But their
existence does not depend upon our knowledge
of them. Nor is the satisfaction of them ren-

dered unreal by our ignorance of the way in which they are satisfied. If God is such a lofty being as the moral ruler of a universe must be, it is not to be expected that we should be able to fathom the necessities which are present to His mind. There must be a world of eternal laws and wants and needs lying about us of which we can form no adequate conception. Into this world Christ entered by His death. Whatever was needed there for the forgiveness and blotting out of man's sin He provided. Whatever the law required for its righteous vindication He performed. It was the Father's will that He should die to redeem men ; and so He died, and men were redeemed.

The foundation of peace.

Thus the atonement appears in the New Testament. Not only from the side of man, but also from the side of God, it is the supremely necessary, and the supremely successful, peace-making sacrifice. "Therefore, being justified by faith, we have peace with God through our Lord Jesus Christ."

IV

Newness of Life

What forgiveness would have been without *What forgiveness brings.*
Christ (if it were possible), no man knows.

What forgiveness is in Christ, what it means
to "have redemption through his blood, even
the forgiveness of sins," — this the gospel that
rings like music through the whole New Testament. It is inward peace, and secret joy, and
newness of life.

An experience like this cannot possibly be
expressed in any language which is fixed and
formal. It must utter itself in vital speech
because it is a vital experience. The attempt
to transform any of the glowing words which
the Apostles use to describe it into a cool, ab-
stract, scientific definition inevitably results in
a misrepresentation. The attempt to interpret
any of the terms which are associated with the
experience of atonement as if they described
legal transactions or artificial adjustments destroys their real significance as utterances of
conscious life.

Take, for example, Paul's famous phrase, *Justifica-*
"justified by faith." Suppose we attempt to *tion by faith.*
define that by making it mean that the guilt

of the sinner has been legally transferred to Christ, and the merits of Christ have been legally transferred to the sinner; so that Christ on the cross is declared guilty and is punished for sin, while the sinner, believing, is pronounced righteous and escapes from punishment. What effect would such an idea of the atonement have upon the inner life? Apart from the frightful confusion which it must introduce into the moral sense to think of God as the author of such an arrangement, what conceivable influence of a real and permanent nature could such a thought have upon the soul? Does it bring inward happiness to a man's heart to be pronounced righteous when he knows that he is still unrighteous? Does it give a man inward peace to be set free from punishment when he is conscious that the evils which deserved it are still within him? Does it reconcile a man's inner life with God to have the righteousness of another person attributed to him by a legal fiction, while his own soul is still out of harmony with God?

No fiction in Christ's mission. Merely to put these questions is to see the answer to them. No; if Christ's mission is to the inner life, then His work in the inner life must be real and vital. In this region there is no room for anything that is merely

formal and artificial. There is no room **for**
what Phillips Brooks calls "the fantastic conception of the imputation to Christ of a sinfulness which was not His, of God's counting
Him guilty of wickedness which He had never
done."

There is no legal fiction in the real atonement.

God is not a maker of fiction, nor can the
inner life of man be satisfied with formalities.
The human heart revolts at the idea of the
punishment of the innocent in the place of the
guilty. Those instincts which lie deeper than
all reasoning, are insulted and wounded by the
thought of the arbitrary transfer of the merits
of one person to the credit of another person.
The moral sense could never find peace in the
contemplation of such a purely forensic trans-
action.

But the testimony of the Apostles is that *Righteous-*
their moral sense, their conscience, actually *ness im-*
did find peace through the atonement as they *parted.*
believed in it. "Justification by faith," as
they use the words, must therefore mean something very different from the definition which
has sometimes been given to it. It must mean
that righteousness is not merely imputed, but
actually imparted through faith. It must mean

that sinners are not merely declared just, but actually made just, by Christ's work as the Saviour. It is not justification of law, it is "justification of life." [1]

A new obedience.

There is not a single passage in the New Testament where the merits of one person are transferred, or reckoned, or counted to another. But there are a hundred passages where the righteousness and obedience of Christ are spoken of as the source of a new righteousness, a new obedience in us. "How much more shall the blood of Christ purge your conscience from dead works to serve the living God." [2]   "Elect according to the foreknowledge of God the Father, through sanctification of the Spirit, unto obedience and sprinkling of the blood of Christ." [3]   "Our Saviour Jesus Christ, who gave himself for us that he might redeem us from all iniquity and purify unto himself a peculiar people, zealous of good works." [4]   "If we walk in the light as he is in the light, we have fellowship one with another, and the blood of Jesus Christ his Son cleanseth us from all sin." [5]

Faith counted unto righteousness.

What, then, does Paul mean when he says that "faith is counted for righteousness"? [6]

[1] Rom. v. 18.   [3] 1 Pet. i. 2.   [5] 1 John i. 7.
[2] Heb. ix. 14.   [4] Titus ii. 14.   [6] Rom. iv. 5.

He means not that faith is taken in the place of righteousness, as if it were enough for a man to believe that Christ was holy without making any effort to attain to holiness himself. He means that faith is regarded as an actual beginning of righteousness, a seed of divine promise and power in the soul of man, to be unfolded, by the grace of God, into a holy life.[1] He means that there is infinitely more hope and potency of goodness in the man who trusts in God's mercy to save him, and in God's holiness to purify him, and in God's grace to make him righteous, than there is in the man who tries to work out salvation in his own strength according to the law. This is Paul's personal consciousness of the atonement. It is not the peace of death : it is the peace of new life joined to God. It involves a spiritual crucifixion with Christ unto sin. It involves also a real resurrection with Christ unto righteousness. "Therefore we are buried with him by baptism into death, that like as Christ was raised up from the dead by the glory of the Father, even so we should walk in newness of life."[2]

[1] Marvin R. Vincent, *Word-Studies in the New Testament*, Vol. III., p. 52.

[2] Rom. vi. 4.

Newness of life, — new hopes, new powers, new inspiration, new courage, — that is the practical side of regeneration. And that, according to the New Testament, is the result of the atonement which Christ brings into the inner life of man.

Paul's legalism. Paul was certainly the one writer among the Apostles who took the most legal point of view in considering the work of Christ. His temperament, his training, inclined him to this method of thought and expression. He was the lawyer of the gospel. But Paul never for a moment dreamed that his forensic figures of speech exhausted or limited the meaning of the gospel.

Nothing could be more absurd, more false to the facts, than to make the message of Paul a mere gospel of escape from the law by belief in the vicarious sacrifice of Christ. Such a view of his gospel would make it and keep it a purely legal gospel. Satisfaction of the law would be still its main theme and motive. It would differ from the religion of the Pharisees only in the way in which it proposed to satisfy the law. It would present a view of justification based upon a different ground indeed, but which in its results, if they did not go beyond escape from the law, would be just as incomplete, just as formal, just as dead, as justification by works.

Paul's message was certainly a gospel of escape from the law; but it was that because it was something infinitely more. It was a gospel of escape into life.

Paul's escape into life.

This was the new birth that came to him when he saw Christ. In the old life his chief concern had been to fulfil the demands of the law; and that was not really a life at all; it was a kind of death, not only because it was a hopeless struggle, but also because it was a subordination of the inward to the outward, of the vital to the formal, of the spirit to the letter. In the new life Paul felt that he was set free from the task of fulfilling the law, not merely because Christ had satisfied all its conceivable demands, but also because Christ had brought him into an utterly different relation to God; not outward, but inward; not formal, but vital; not artificial, but spiritual.

Paul's message was more than a doctrine of law satisfied in Christ. It was a proclamation of life begun in Christ. There was as much righteousness in this new life as there was in the old law. But it was a new kind of righteousness. Certainly it was not a fictitious

The new kind of righteousness.

kind of righteousness, a mere legal justification, a formal transfer of the merits of Christ,
by some mysterious decree of a supreme court,
to the credit of the believer. It was a real
righteousness, living and working itself out
in the life of man. But it differed from the
old righteousness in two things. First, in its
origin: it was not human, but divine; and
therefore it must be received by faith. Second, in its operation: it was not conformity
to a rule, but guidance by the Spirit; and
therefore it must be perfected by love.

Salvation through life.   Paul's teaching amounts to this. We are
not saved through law; we are saved through
life. Life does not mean outward obedience.
That is only the shell of life. Real life means
faith and hope and love. The only source
of this life is in God. Christ alone brings
this life near to us, makes it accessible, sweeps
away all hindrances, and invites us to enter
into it by giving ourselves entirely to him.
To live, according to Paul, means to believe
in Christ, to hope in Christ, and to love
Christ, because He is the human life of God,
"delivered for our offences and raised again
for our justification." [1]

Mark well the words. Why "*raised again*

[1] Rom. iv. 25.

for our justification ? " If the taking away of our sins means only the release from their punishment because He has borne them upon the cross, then His resurrection makes no difference in the result. If our justification means only the imputation of the merit of His obedience and the value of His sacrifice to our account, then His rising again from the dead has nothing to do with it. Everything would be secure, whether He rose, or whether He did not rise.

Why *"raised again for our justification?"* Because the taking away of our sins means an actual separation from sin by union with the crucified Christ. Because our justification means a living entrance into His righteousness in the risen life. The mission of Christ to the inner life was just this : To make such an atonement that sin should no more divide the soul from God : To make such an atonement that the broken law should no more keep the soul at enmity with God : To make such an atonement that the inner life of all who truly live, should be "not unto themselves, but unto him who died for them and rose again."

V

THE PERFECTION OF ATONEMENT

We may not know, we cannot tell,
  What pains He had to bear;
But we believe it was for us
  He hung and suffered there.

He died that we might be forgiven;
  He died to make us good,
That we might go at last to heaven
  Saved by His precious blood.

—CECIL FRANCES ALEXANDER.

V

THE PERFECTION OF ATONEMENT

ATONEMENT is the word that seems best *The atone-ment not to be defined.* fitted to express the meaning of the gospel of Christ in relation to a world of sin. I have used it thus far without defining it, for three reasons.

First, because a final definition is impossible. The work of Christ for the saving of sinners can never be confined within the phrases which men invent to describe what they can see of it. It overflows the boundaries. Its fulness makes it indefinable.

Second, because the very attempt to define *Of the making of many books.* it has so often led to misconception and strife between men who believed in it with equal sincerity. I have read many books on the atonement. If the titles and references were given here, they would fill several pages. In almost all of these books I have found truth; in none of them the whole truth. The writers have helped me most when they have expressed their own experience of the saving

131

power of Christ.   They have helped me least
when they have been making definitions to
shut out and condemn the views of other
writers.   Yet even in this they have not been
altogether unprofitable.   An attack upon a
book has often led me to read it sympatheti-
cally, and so to discover in it a new source
of illumination, a new testimony of experience.

Clearness without definition.   The third reason why I have not tried to
give a definition of the atonement is because
it is not needed.   The word is clear enough
and plain enough already.   It denotes a certain mystery, — the entire work of Christ in
reuniting man to God, — the perfect result of
that work in the establishment of peace between man and God, — the redeeming relation
of that work to human sin, — the satisfying
relation of that work to divine righteousness,
— it denotes a mystery, but it denotes it in
language which brings it into analogy with
things that we know, and throws upon it light
enough to enable us to see at least some of its
essential elements.

The history of the word.   For what is this word, and where does it
come from?   It comes directly out of human
life and experience.   It is derived from an
older word, "*onement*," which means unity or

concord.[1]   To set two persons or things "at onement" means to bring them together in harmony after discord.   Atonement is simply the process, or the result, of reuniting and reconciling those who have been separated. Thus, in Shakespeare's *Richard III.*, Buckingham says to the Queen:

> "Ay, madame; he desires to make atonement
> Between the Duke of Gloster and your brothers."

From this original and broadest meaning, the word is sometimes narrowed a little to denote some particular action or offering by which the reconciliation is effected.   It may come either from one of the separated parties, or from a third person who offers himself as a reconciler. But in any case three elements must always enter into the idea of an atonement.

First, the motive of it must be love.   It cannot possibly spring from any other cause. Justice, or righteousness, or authority, — and least of all anger or hate, — would never account for the desire of making a reconciliation.   It can only come from a sincere love

Three elements in all atonement.

---

[1] "Ye witless gallants, I beshrew your hearts
Which make such discord 'twixt agreeing parts,
Which never can be set at onement more."
BISHOP HALL's *Satires*, 1599.

for the persons to be reconciled, and an earnest wish that they shall love each other.

Second, the condition under which this love works is the sense of a present separation, arising out of a fault, an offence, which has created a real obstacle between the persons who are in enmity.

Third, the purpose which this love has in view is a real state of harmony, in which the persons who are to be brought together shall be vitally at one.

These, then, are the three marks of all atonement. Its creative cause is the power of love. Its occasional cause is the recognition of an offence. Its final cause is the restoration of vital union.

Lesser atonements. Atonements have been going on in the world from the beginning; between man and man, and between man and God. Those who have been conscious of injury and offence against their fellow-men have been trying to make some reparation, to show some contrition for the wrong, and to reëstablish peace. Those who have been grieved at the prevalence of enmity and strife among their friends have been trying to bring about reconciliation, by mediating between the offended and the offender.

This mediation involves suffering and sacrifice on the part of the peacemaker. It is hardly possible to obtain forgiveness and love for a guilty person without bearing something of his pain and punishment. Many a father has suffered for the sake of making peace among his children who were at strife. Many a mother has borne not only grief, but also actual trouble and loss, for the sake of reconciling a rebellious boy to an offended father. Many a brother has shared the disgrace and paid the debts of a brother, for the sake of bringing him back into the harmony of the social order. And in such sufferings of love for the cause of atonement there is always something which propitiates the heart and inclines it to show favour. The father's compassion toward an erring son is always deepened and quickened by the thought of the mother's love as expressed in sacrifice. The sentiment of society, which after all is the final earthly court of appeal in all questions of conduct, is certainly affected favourably toward an offender by the fact that an innocent friend is willing to stand beside him and share in some degree the consequences of his fault. All this is of the nature of atonement, and there is no corner of the world where the letters of this word may not be spelled out, like a dim and broken inscription, on the fragments of human life.

Sacrifices for sin.

The same word runs through the history of religion from the beginning until now. Sacrifice is another way of spelling it; and sacrifice is primitive and universal.

"Both for themselves and those who call them friend" men have not only prayed, but also presented gifts and offerings to God, in the desire to take away the obstacle of sin and reconcile the human heart to Him.

Atonement in the Old Testament.

Atonement is spoken of in the Old Testament in many places. It is said that an atonement was made when Moses interceded for the people at Sinai,[1] when Aaron burned incense in the midst of the congregation,[2] when Phinehas executed judgment on Zimri,[3] and when Nehemiah established ordinances in the restored city of Jerusalem.[4] The Hebrew word which is used in these passages, and in many others where some form of the verb "to atone" occurs in our English version, is from a root which means "to cover." It carries with it the idea of guilt which needs to be expiated. But the object of the expiation is the renewal of fellowship between man and God. Sacrifice has this twofold meaning. The slaying of the victim is the confession that sin deserves punishment.

[1] Ex. xxxii. 30.
[2] Num. xvi. 46.
[3] Num. xxv. 13.
[4] Neh. x. 33.

The offering of the blood, which is the sign of the life, is the utterance of the worshipper's desire to return into union with God.[1]

Now all these kinds of atonement, which men *The figures of the true.* have been making through the centuries, and are making still, are but shadows and reflections of the great work which Christ came to do for a sinful world. Its purpose and design, its nature and conditions, the depth of its motive and the breadth of its scope, cannot be expressed by any lesser, narrower, more precise word.

It takes up into itself the significance of all *The final sacrifice.* sincere and pure sacrifices which have been offered on human altars, visible and invisible. Christ is the eternal embodiment of the sacrificial spirit.[2]

It utters the great peace-making desire of *The great Peace-maker.* all those blessed human mediators who have laboured and suffered to bring together divided hearts and to restore harmony between discordant lives.[3] In this light it reveals Christ as standing between God and man, and touching both the human and the divine.

It is the perfect consummation of all those *The High Priest of mankind.* imperfect offerings which have been made in

[1] *Lux Mundi*, pp. 279 ff.   [2] Heb. ix. 26.
[3] Eph. ii. 14–18.

behalf of those who are guilty, to propitiate One who has a right to be offended with them. In this sense Christ appears as the High Priest of sinful and repentant humanity.[1]

The forgiving heart of God.   It is the divine interpretation and consecration of all those royal acts of compassion and mercy in which men and women who have been sinned against have expressed their free forgiveness and sought to win their enemies back to peace.   In this aspect Christ is revealed as the incarnate love of God, coming forth from the bosom of the Father, to seek and to save His lost children.[2]

No word which fails to cover all these meanings, no word which sharply emphasizes one side of the truth at the expense of the other sides, no word which leaves out of its significance the sweetness of any of those things most "pure and lovely and of good report" which have been done in the spirit of reconciliation, is broad enough to describe the work of Christ in closing the gulf which sin had made between man and God.   Sacrifice is not broad enough. Mediation is not broad enough.   Propitiation is not broad enough.   Redemption is not broad enough.   Substitution is not broad enough. Satisfaction is not broad enough.   Embracing

[1] Heb. x. 10–14.   [2] 1 John iii. 16.

all these things, Christ's work goes beyond
them all. It is simply the perfection of atonement.

The word occurs but once in the English *"Atone-*
version of the New Testament, in a passage *ment" in*
where St. Paul declares that "we joy in God *Testament.*
through our Lord Jesus Christ, by whom we
have now received the atonement."[1] But the
same Greek noun which is here rendered
"atonement," occurs again in a later verse,
where he speaks of "the reconciling of the
world,"[2] and in a still more important passage
of another epistle, where he describes the gospel as "the word of the reconciliation," and the
preacher's work as "the ministry of the reconciliation."[3] The translation should be made
uniform in all three places. Then we should
have "the atonement of the world," "the word
of the atonement," and "the ministry of the
atonement."

This would prepare us to appreciate the full *The classic*
force of another passage in which we find, not *passage.*
the noun, but the verb from which it is derived, in an intensive form which gives it new
value, and in a connection which seems to pour
fresh light upon it from all sides of human

[1] Rom. v. 11.   [2] Rom. xi. 15.
[3] 2 Cor. v. 18, 19.

experience.[1]   The classic passage on the atonement is in the first chapter of the Epistle to the
Colossians, and the central idea of it is in the
twentieth verse, in which St. Paul declares
that it pleased the Father, by Christ, " to atone
all things with himself; by him, I say, whether
they be things in earth, or things in heaven."
Go backward and forward from this point, and
see how many meanings converge in St. Paul's
idea of the great atonement.   Deliverance from
the power of darkness ;[2] redemption through
Christ's blood, even the forgiveness of sins ;[3]
a new birth from the dead ;[4] peace-making by
the cross ;[5] the winning back of enemies ;[6]
the taking away of blame and reproof ;[7] the
interpretation of human sufferings in fellowship with the afflictions of Christ ;[8] and finally
the making known of the riches of the glory
of a mystery, " which is Christ in you, the hope
of glory."[9]   This, indeed, is atonement made
perfect.

*When that
which is
perfect is
come.*
   The perfection of it lies in the fulness and
clearness with which it embodies and expresses
the three essential elements of all lesser atone-

---

[1] The noun is κατάλλαγη : the verb is καταλλάσσω : the
intensive form is ἀποκαταλλάττω.

[2] vs. 13.   [3] vs. 14.   [4] vs. 18.   [5] vs. 20.   [6] vs. 21.
[7] vs. 22.   [8] vs. 24.   [9] vs. 27.

ments. Its purpose is a true, deep, eternal harmony of spirit between man and God, a peace which the world can neither give nor take away. Its condition of operative power is a full acknowledgment of the immense obstacle which sin has put between man and God. Its motive is pure and perfect love, — the love which meets all needs as man feels them in his repentant heart, — the love which passeth knowledge in its power to cover the whole mystery of sin as it is known to God alone.

The Love that meets All Needs

Atonement begins with God's love.

There is no truly Christian view of the atonement which does not begin with the love of God.[1] This love involves the primal purpose of self-revelation, of fellowship with man, of a divine incarnation. There is a gospel, a promise of God's communication of Himself to man, in the very act of creation. " The faith of the atonement presupposes the faith of the incarnation." [2]

If this be true, it follows that we may believe that the Son of God would have come into the world whether man had sinned or not. God has chosen and loved mankind in His Son before the foundation of the world.[3] There is a profound truth in the saying of Robertson of Brighton, " God's idea of humanity is, *and ever was*, humanity as it is in Jesus Christ." [4]

Atonement a form of Incarnation.

Atonement, therefore, is the form which is given to the incarnation by the presence of sin

[1] Charles Cuthbert Hall, *The Gospel of the Divine Sacrifice*, ch. i.
[2] Campbell, *The Nature of the Atonement*, pp. xvi ff.
[3] Eph. i. 4.
[4] *Life and Letters of F. W. Robertson*, Vol. II., p. 121.

in the world. Christ would have come to us
as the revealer of the divine love, even though
the world had never been separated from God.[1]
But because the separation had actually taken
place, because man had offended against God,
and departed from His ideal, and fallen into
enmity with Him, Christ must reveal the
divine love as a suffering love, a sacrificial
love, a reconciling love, in order to bring man
back to God.

This atoning form of incarnation appears to *The glory of*
us more glorious, more wonderful, than any *this form.*
other form, because it costs more. It is love
put to the test. It is love overcoming ob-
stacles. It is love militant and victorious.
And its perfection is manifest in the freedom
and fulness with which it meets all the needs
imposed by the fact of sin.

Our consciousness of these needs is the *The known*
measure of our power to understand the atone- *and the un-*
ment. But beyond this consciousness there is *known.*
another region wherein the results of evil, the
disorders which it has introduced into the world,
surpass our comprehension. In that region we
cannot fully understand the atonement. We

[1] Westcott's *Commentary on the Epistles of John*, pp.
273 ff. Oxenham, *The Catholic Doctrine of the Atonement*,
pp. 80 ff.

can only accept it, and rest upon it, as a great fact through which the concord of an untuned universe is restored, and infinite mercy is harmonized with infinite justice in the redemptive government of the world.

In music there are notes too high and too low for us to hear. But the chord which fills the range of our hearing with harmony must be harmonious also in the unheard undertones and overtones. Our faith in the unmeasured values of the atonement in the spheres beyond our ken is inseparably connected with an experience of its active power to meet our conscious wants as sinful men.

The needs of sinners.   What are these wants? They spring from the four elements which are present in the sense of sin,—the shame of impurity, the pain of bondage, the apprehension of guilt, and the hope of mercy.[1] To these four elements, and to the needs which arise out of them, there are four things in the atonement which correspond, —a power to cleanse the soul, a power to liberate the life, a power to satisfy the law, and a power to reveal forgiveness. And these four things are spoken of in the New Testament under four principal expressions, —a sin-offer-

[1] Ch. ii., pp. 40 ff.

ing;[1] a ransom;[2] a satisfaction, the payment of a debt;[3] and a reconciliation.[4]

There is a famous passage in Coleridge's *Aids to Reflection*[5] in which he explains that these expressions are figures of speech, which do not describe the real nature of the atonement, but only illustrate "the nature and extent of the consequences and effects of the atonement, and excite in the receivers a due sense of the magnitude and manifold operation of the boon, and of the love and gratitude due to the Redeemer." *Metaphors of the atonement.*

I should accept the positive part of Coleridge's explanation, but I should reject the negative part of it.

Undoubtedly these metaphors are intended to express the great benefits which sinners receive from the atoning work of Christ. They describe the results which it produces in the consciousness of man, — a sense of cleansing from defilement, a sense of deliverance from slavery, a sense of being right with the law, and a sense of God's willingness to *Their reality.*

---

[1] Heb. ix. 19–28 ; 1 John i. 7 ; Rev. i. 5.
[2] 1 Tim. ii. 6; Gal. iv. 5 ; Eph. i. 7; Col. i. 14.
[3] Gal. v. 3 ; 2 Cor. v. 21 ; 1 Pet. iii. 18.
[4] Eph. ii. 14, 16 ; 2 Tim. ii. 5.
[5] pp. 309 ff., American edition.

pardon. These are subjective effects. They are within us. But do they not belong to the real nature and intention of the atonement? Are they not clear indications of its purpose and meaning? Is not this complete reconciliation with God, in spite of sin, precisely what it was intended to accomplish? Are not these consequences in man's spiritual consciousness just as real, just as veritable, as any other consequences that we can imagine?

The meeting-point. The atonement, as has been said, "is the meeting-point of the objective and subjective elements of Christianity."[1] It covers all the ground that lies between God and man, so far as sin has touched it. It has a reference to every element of the divine nature which condemus sin, and to every element of human nature which is affected by sin. It acts directly upon the divine will and upon the human will.[2] There is no possible metaphor, drawn from any real relation of man to God, which is without its value in illustrating the real nature of the atonement.

So far, then, from denying the verity of these four figures of speech, we should accept

[1] Oxenham, *Catholic Doctrine of the Atonement*, p. xl.
[2] Ritschl, *History of the Christian Doctrine of Justification and Reconciliation*, p. 9.

them as expressions of substantial truth. We should seek to make them as real and living as possible in our own experience. And we should go back to the New Testament to see if there are not other metaphors of the atonement which fit in with our consciousness of need as sinners.

There are four other figures of speech, less familiar, and less frequently used, which throw new light upon the subject. They are used by Christ Himself to describe the effects of His sacrifice. It would be well if they were taken more deeply into our conception of the atonement. *The figures used by Christ.*

The first figure is the metaphor of germination. "Except a corn of wheat fall into the ground and die, it abideth alone: but if it die, it bringeth forth much fruit."[1] This means that Christ's death is the means of communicating new life — pure, holy, immortal — to the souls of men. It answers to the need which springs out of the shame of sin as the conscious deadening of the higher life. *Germination.*

The second figure is the metaphor of vicarious suffering. "I am the good shepherd: the good shepherd giveth his life for the sheep."[2] This means that because Christ loves us, and *The Shepherd dying for the sheep.*

[1] John xii. 24.   [2] John x. 11.

has identified Himself with us, He is willing to die for us in order to rescue us from sin, the robber of our souls. It is another aspect of redemption, the ransom of a life willingly laid down for others in the conflict with evil. It answers to the painful sense of helplessness in our struggles to escape from sin. It is the voice of the victor who stands by the vanquished and promises deliverance.

Consecration. The third figure is the metaphor of consecration. "For their sakes I sanctify myself, that they also might be sanctified through the truth."[1] This means that Christ's death is the completion of His holy obedience to God. It is more than the payment of a debt exacted by the law. It is the fulfilment of a service prompted by love. "Lo, I come to do thy will, O God."[2] And so it becomes in us the spirit of a new obedience.

The new covenant. The fourth figure is the metaphor of a new covenant of pardon. "This is my blood of the new covenant, which is shed for many for the remission of sins."[3] This means that Christ's death is the seal of God's entering into a new engagement with us, not of works, but of grace, in which He will deal with us as a

[1] John xvii. 19.   [2] Heb. x. 9.
[3] Matt. xxvi. 28.

father, forgiving our sins for His name's sake.
An ancient covenant was always sealed with
blood. But it was not made on account of the
blood. That was simply the sign of the solem-
nity and binding force of the engagement. The
covenant itself rested upon the willingness of
both parties to enter into it and to keep it.
Christ's death does not make God willing to
forgive. It reveals His forgiveness as ready
and waiting for us to claim it.

Now take these four latter metaphors of the *A com-parison.*
effects of the atonement in its relation to us,
and lay them beside the four others which are
more familiarly employed. See how they mu-
tually illuminate one another, and how the
light which comes from each reminds us that
no one of them can be interpreted alone as
the secret of "the true doctrine of atonement."

There is a sacrificial element in it, assuredly. *The sacrificial element.*
It is an offering for sin. But it is not in
any sense an offering which is separate from
us. It is implanted in us, in our human nature,
as a seed is planted in the earth, to germinate
and bear fruit.

There was a substitution on Calvary. But
it was not the substitution of a sinless Christ
for a sinful race. It was the substitution of

humanity *plus* Christ, for humanity *minus* Christ. He bore our sins, not apart from us, but with us. He expressed, in His willing submission to the death of the cross, the ideal and representative repentance of mankind for sin.[1] And this sacrifice is the sufficient atonement for the original sin of the whole race. He is joined by His cross to every sinful soul that repents of actual sin, and thus there is no further need of sacrifice, since the offering of Christ abides forever and germinates in each heart that believes in Him. To be crucified with Christ is to feel the guilt of sin in like manner (though never in like degree) as He felt it. It is to acknowledge the righteousness of the law which condemns sin, even as He acknowledged it by suffering with the race which lay under condemnation. It is to present to God, by faith, our lesser sacrifices of a broken and a contrite spirit, not now standing alone in their imperfection, but purified and made precious by union with that perfect sacrifice in which Jesus Christ poured out His soul unto death.

The redemptive element. There is also a redemptive element in the atonement, undoubtedly. It is a ransom which

[1] Campbell, *The Nature of the Atonement*, pp. 247 ff.

emancipates us from the tyranny of evil. But
it is not, as the patristic writers imagined, a
ransom paid to the devil. There is no trace
of such an idea in the New Testament. It is,
as Christ Himself teaches us, a victory over the
evil one. It is our ransom, just as the death of a
heroic leader who conquers in a good cause and
in conquering dies, is the ransom of his people
from defeat and slavery. The liberating power
of Christ's death for us is never to be separated
from His spiritual victory over evil, nor from
the courage which it inspires in our hearts to
know that we have such a mighty, faithful,
triumphant Shepherd.

There is also an element of satisfaction to *The satis-*
the righteous law in the atonement, undoubt-   *faction.*
edly. Christ fulfilled all that the law of God
required. He paid the debt of righteousness
to the full. But the emphasis in this satisfaction is not to be laid exclusively, nor chiefly,
upon His sufferings, but upon His holiness,
upon His willing and complete obedience to
the Father in all things. As St. Bernard said,
Non mors, sed voluntas placuit sponte morientis.
The value and meaning of Christ's atonement as a satisfaction depends upon the connection of His sufferings and death with His

perfect life. It was "the mind that was in Christ Jesus" that made Him "obedient unto death, even the death of the cross."[1] That mind of obedience was the priceless jewel worth more than enough to pay the whole debt of righteousness.

If Christ had died in childhood? The truth of this view is self-evident. How can we think of it in any other way ? Suppose for a moment that Christ had died in infancy. Suppose that instead of escaping into Egypt with the Virgin Mary and St. Joseph, the babe Jesus had been slain with the other children of Bethlehem. His death would still have been the sacrifice of an innocent victim. It would still have shown the hatefulness and cruelty of human sin. It might still be regarded, in imagination, as the substitution of the guiltless for the guilty. It might still be defined, by a legal fiction, as the transference of a penalty to one who had not transgressed. It might still be presented, by a purely forensic theory, as an exhibition of a supposed vindictive element in the law, which could only be satisfied by the shedding of innocent blood. All this might still be attributed to the death of Christ if it had befallen Him in helpless infancy. But would it then have been, in any satisfactory

[1] Phil. ii. 5–8.

sense, an atoning sacrifice? Would it have had any power to really reconcile our hearts with the law which requires righteousness?

No, a thousand times no! That which gives *The value of obedience.* the obedience of the cross its reconciling power is the fact that it was voluntary suffering, holy suffering, suffering which made Christ perfect,[1] the crown and consummation of His patient, faithful, self-denying, stainless life.

It is only when we look at it in this way that the holiness of Christ becomes, not the substitute for our holiness (which would contradict the spirit of the law), but the source of our holiness,[2] — the consecration of our Kinsman High-Priest, in which and by which the consecration of His brethren is secured.[3] "Christ is the end of the law for righteousness to every one that believeth."[4] Thus, and thus only, the law is satisfied in Him.

Once more, there is a reconciling element in *The reconciliation.* the atonement, undoubtedly. It does remove a real obstacle between man and God. It does bring God nearer to man, in order that man may come close to God. But this obstacle is

[1] Heb. ii. 10.
[2] W. E. Gladstone, *Later Gleanings*, p. 336.
[3] Heb. ii. 11-18.   [4] Rom. x. 4.

never to be thought of as an unwillingness on God's part to pardon and restore the guilty. This reconciliation is always to be interpreted in the light of Christ's word of "the new covenant," freely and gladly made by the divine mercy, and sealed with the most holy seal in the universe, —"the precious blood of Christ, as of a lamb without blemish and without spot." [1]

Grace is the cause of atonement.

The atonement, then, is never to be regarded as the cause of God's grace. It is the result and the seal of His grace. It is the channel made by grace, through which all the blessed effects of the divine love may flow, across the bitter waste that sin has made, to all who hunger and thirst after righteousness, in order that they may be filled.

What has it done for you?

If any one should ask, therefore, "What has the atonement done for you?" our answer should be broad enough to cover all our needs. With Christ God has freely given us all things : an assurance of mercy, divinely sealed ; a satisfaction of the law, divinely perfected ; a ransom from evil, divinely accomplished ; a sacrifice for sin, divinely offered ; a covenant of peace ; a spirit of consecration ; a good Shepherd of our souls ; a seed of everlasting life, — and if

[1] 1 Pet. i. 19.

there be any other thing that sinners need for
their salvation, doubtless this also is waiting
to be discovered in the atonement.

The only false view is that which questions
the reality of any of these blessings.   The only
dangerous view is that which interprets any
one of them in such a way as to make it merely
formal and artificial, and to deny the necessity
of the others.   All views are true which recognize, through experience, the love of God in
Christ meeting any of our needs as sinful men,
and which preserve a grateful openness of heart
to welcome every new ray of light that comes
from the cross through the experience of other
men.

After all is said, out of the fulness of each *The un-*
ransomed heart, there still remains a secret *speakable*
reason for gratitude, unuttered because not yet *gift.*
perfectly realized.   "Thanks be unto God **for**
his unspeakable gift."[1]

[1] 2 Cor. ix. 15.

II

The Love that passeth Knowledge

The twofold mystery.   If there is a mystery in sin, there must also be a mystery in the atonement.[1]

We can know the love of God in Christ which meets all our conscious needs as sinners. But that love, as it makes provision for all the unsearchable necessities of God's moral government of the universe, must be a love that passeth knowledge.

There are some theologians who object strenuously to this acknowledgment of a mystery in the atonement.   It seems to them that it leaves "in the very focus of revelation a spot of pure impenetrable black."[2]   I would rather say that it leaves a centre of "light inaccessible and full of glory."

The humility of partial knowledge is not the same as the despair of total ignorance.   "We know in part, and we prophesy in part."[3]   This was the last text from which President James McCosh spoke in the chapel of Princeton University.   "We know in part," said he ; "*but we know!*"

[1] Ch. ii., p. 26.
[2] James Denney, *Studies in Theology*, p. 106.
[3] 1 Cor. xiii. 9.

We know sin, for example, in its qualities *Sin only* and results, since they are manifested in human *partly known.* life and in our own souls. But we do not perfectly know it; for its origin, and the secret forces which keep it alive and operative, though it be in itself a kind of death, and the strange subterranean relations which give it a unity amid all its diversity, and the mysterious power by which it destroys freedom of will while seeming to express it, — these things are hidden from us. They are inscrutable. Sin is a bottomless gulf. To account for it rationally would be to justify its existence. "Sin explained," said Dr. Edward G. Robinson, "would be sin defended." It is in fact a kind of reversed miracle. It is the action of the creature without the creator. It takes place in a sphere below the reach of our thought. It transcends reason, — *downward.*

It is fitting, therefore, it is altogether to be *Atonement* expected, that the atonement which is to *inexplicable.* take away sin should also transcend reason, — but *upward.* It ought to be, as it is, an inexplicable and unsearchable mystery of redeeming love, just as sin is an inexplicable and unsearchable mystery of enslaving hate. It ought to cover, as it does, all those secret relations in which the unity of righteousness consists, just as sin entangles the soul in that network of subtle bondage wherein the unity of evil consists. The atonement, in its divine essence, must go as far above our knowledge, as sin, in its mortal perversity, goes below it.

Mercy and justice.   Consider the subject from another point of view. The atonement is undoubtedly the manifestation of God's mercy in harmony with His justice. But what is mercy, and what is justice, in our knowledge of them, but fragments of a great circle which sweeps far beyond our vision. So far as logic goes, the forgiveness of sins appears like an absolutely impossible thing. An offence once committed must stand on the books forever as a thing to be condemned and punished. So far as logic goes, the execution of absolute justice seems to be equally impossible. We have never seen it. We cannot conceive nor explain it. "Justice is a fragment, mercy is a fragment, mediation is a fragment; justice, mercy, mediation as a reason of mercy — all three; what indeed are they but great vistas and openings into an invisible world in which is the point of view which brings them all together."[1]

And yet in this mysterious region into which

[1] Mozley's *University Sermons*, p. 177.

the divine side of the atonement reaches, there are two things which we ought to believe, even though we cannot fully comprehend them. *Two points are clear.*

First, it is necessary to the reality of faith to believe that the atonement has a practical relation to God, an actual and direct effect upon the divine will as well as upon our will. "Christ's work can be regarded as efficacious in the justification and reconciliation of men only in so far as we, at the same time, recognize a reference of that work to God. Nay, rather, His saving operations upon men cannot be understood except it be presupposed that His doing and suffering for that end had also a value for God, whether that be expressed in the notions of satisfaction, merit, propitiation, or somehow otherwise." [1]

Second, it is essential to the moral integrity of faith that we should believe that the divine justice and mercy, which are harmonized in the atonement, are not different in kind, but only in degree, from mercy and justice as they are revealed in our fragmentary knowledge. There can be no satisfaction of divine justice which does not justify itself in the moral sense. There can be no propitiation of mercy which introduces

- [1] Ritschl, *History of the Christian Doctrine of Justification, etc.*, p. 9.

a conflict, or an appearance of conflict, among the attributes of God.   Mercy must be merciful; and justice, just.

Immoral analogies shut out.
    This shuts out at once the possibility of interpreting the mystery of atonement by analogy with ideas and figures drawn from imperfect and cruel systems of human government, or from corrupt and superstitious systems of religion.   The notion of a God whose vindictive anger demands a precise equivalent of suffering as the condition of release from penalty does not belong to Christianity.   It belongs to the moral ill-temper of a civilization which, like that of the middle ages or of the sixteenth and seventeenth centuries, was essentially harsh and cruel.   It belongs to a conception of life in which law was relentless and vindictive, — in which men were hung for petty larceny and burned alive for heresy; in which war was simply a colossal public revenge, and a captured city was certain to be sacked.   It belongs, in its religious kinship, to paganism, to fetichism, to the cruel, sensual religions of Mexico and Africa.

False phrases of theology.
    Shadows of their darkness have fallen upon the outer form of Christianity.   Strange and uncouth words have found their way into the dogmatic books which vainly seek to reduce

life to logic. Wild and wandering phrases of
bewildered theologians have represented Christ
as exposed to the divine wrath in our place, or
as "wiping away the red anger-spot from the
brow of God." Dismal echoes from the chants
of blood-stained heathen temples have crept
into the hymns of the church, — echoes which
say that

> "On Christ Almighty vengeance fell
> Which must have sunk a world to hell,"

or that

> "One rosy drop from Jesus' heart
> Was worlds of seas to quench God's ire."

These echoes, these phrases, these words, have
undoubtedly penetrated, in a wavering and un-
certain way, into the ritual, the dogma, the
outer circle, of Christianity. It seems as if, to
use the expression of that great German theologian, Rothe, "in His work for man it were
the constant fate of God to be misunderstood."
But these misunderstandings cannot enter, and
they have not entered, into the inner life where
Christ is truly manifested as the living sacrifice
and Saviour.

There is not a word in all the New Testament
which implies that Christ offered a sacrifice to
the anger of God. It is morally inconceivable

*Christ was
never under
God's wrath.*

M

that the Redeemer coming from the bosom of
the Father to do His work should ever have
been, in any sense, an object of the divine wrath.
For that wrath, as we have already seen, is not
a vindictive anger against sinners; it is a pure
and holy indignation against sin. How, then,
could it have rested for a single moment upon
Christ?

Nor is there anything in the Bible to imply
that Christ has taken that wrath against sin
away. It still exists. It still hates and condemns sin as much as ever.

Christ delivers us from the fear of it, not by
subjecting Himself to it, but by separating us
from the sin against which it is directed.

How, then, shall we interpret Christ's sufferings?

*How did
Christ
suffer?*
There was no infliction of punishment upon
the innocent instead of the guilty. There was
no transference of the demerits of the sinful to
the sinless. Christ remained guiltless; man
remained guilty. But Christ entered into humanity, freely, willingly, taking on Himself all
its limitations, burdens, pains, and sorrows.
Christ lived and died with man and for man.
He was not merely a substitute: He was a
representative. He was not thrust into our
place: He shared our lot; and if that sharing

involved a sacrificial death upon the cross, if there was no other way in which He could be one with sinners, and make them one with Himself, and lift them out of guilt and doom, save by dying for their sins, what then?

Does the recognition of this, as a mysterious fact revealed in the crucifixion, cast any stain upon the justice of God? Not so thought Christ, who shrank from the cross, yet said, "Father, not my will, but thine be done." Not so thought the Apostles, who saw in Christ crucified the perfect revelation of the righteousness and love of God. Not so thought such a Christian as Phillips Brooks. The inner life of Christendom finds a true expression in his sermon on *The Conqueror from Edom*.

"My friends," he says, "far be it from me to read all the deep mystery that is in this picture. Only this I know is the burden and soul of it all, this truth, that sin is a horrible, strong, positive thing, and that not even Divinity grapples with him and subdues him except in strife and pain. What pain may mean to the Infinite and Divine, what difficulty may mean to Omnipotence, I cannot tell. Only I know that all that they could mean, they mean here. This symbol of the blood bears this great truth, which has been the power of salvation to mill-

ions of hearts, and which must make this conqueror the Saviour of your hearts, too, the truth
that only in self-sacrifice and suffering could
even God conquer sin. Sin is never so dreadful as when we see the Saviour with that blood
upon His garments. And the Saviour Himself
is never so dear, never wins so utter and so
tender a love, as when we see what it has cost
Him to save us. Out of that love, born of His
holy suffering, comes the new impulse after a
holy life ; and so, when we stand at last purified
by the power of grateful obedience, binding our
holiness and escape from our sin close to our
Lord's struggle with sin for us, it shall be said
of us that we have ' washed our robes and made
them white in the blood of the Lamb.' " [1]

Divine justice satisfied.

That the divine mercy is satisfied in this
conception of the atonement, no one can doubt.
But how is the satisfaction of the divine justice
manifested in this view ? What glimpse does
it give us of a holy law vindicated, an eternal
righteousness maintained ?

It seems to me that it certainly shows us one
thing, however much it leaves still hidden from
our knowledge in the unsearchable counsels of
God. It shows us that God so honours and
upholds the moral law by which He governs

[1] Phillips Brooks, *Sermons*, Vol. I., p. 53.

the world, that not even Christ could come into union with humanity, not even Christ could become man, without sharing the consequences of man's sin. Christ was not punished for sins that He had never done. Christ was not punished for our sins. Christ was not punished at all. But because our sins deserve punishment, Christ, having become one with us, endured the shame and the cross, poured out His soul unto death and was numbered with the transgressors, suffered and died as the human life of God, because suffering and death have justly come upon the world of sin.

This is indeed the noblest vindication of the law that we can possibly conceive. It elevates and illuminates the atonement, so that it shines far above us, as a supreme mountain-peak of self-consistent righteousness. It makes it a part of an eternal moral order, resting upon the very nature of God, and His relation to the world as its moral governor. It is a doctrine of majesty and power.

Forgiveness without atonement, if we could conceive of such a thing, would leave us far more in the dark, would present a far greater mystery. But forgiveness with atonement assures us that God is in eternal harmony with His own law. He has not permitted suffering

Forgiveness with atonement.

and death to come into the world merely to execute a personal vengeance on sin as an insult offered to His majesty. They are the expression of an eternal and righteous mode of government. Their presence is necessary, and just, and consistent with God's goodness and love as well as with His wisdom and holiness. The Son of God, entering the world to redeem it, not from without but from within, must submit to these conditions.

He could not be punished. That was impossible. But He could suffer and die. And so He did, confessing and glorifying the integrity and solidarity of God's attributes in the moral law of the universe.[1]

A mystery of glory. Wherein that solidarity consists, what is the eternal fitness and propriety of atonement by sacrifice and suffering, we can neither fully understand nor perfectly explain. "The nature of the redemptive act in itself is not to be compassed nor uttered by the language of human understanding."[2] When we look upon it "we are in the presence of forces which issue from infinity, and pass out of our sight even while we are contemplating their effects."[3]

[1] Rom. iii. 25.
[2] Shairp, *Studies in Poetry and Philosophy*, p. 197.
[3] *Lux Mundi*, pp. 285, 310.

This confession of something beyond our comprehension in the atonement runs through all the literature of the Christian religion. Some of the theologians, indeed, scoff at it and reject it. But the heart of the church has always felt it profoundly, and acknowledged it with adoration. On Calvary we behold the "love of Christ which passeth knowledge." [1]

In the present state of our knowledge, the result of attempting to define and explain the atonement thoroughly, is to make it narrower and less attractive to our hearts. To beings such as we are, the full meaning of the cross can be made perfectly plain only at the cost of making it less precious. We know that we need more than we can know. The cross is most dear to our hearts because it is the sign of an unsearchable mystery of saving love.

[1] Eph. iii. 19.

VI

THE MESSAGE OF THE CROSS

Weepers, come to this God, for He doth weep;
Ye sufferers, come to Him, for He doth care;
Ye tremblers, come, for He doth mercy keep;
Come, ye who die, for He doth still endure.

—Victor Hugo,
Écrit au Bas d'un Crucifix, 1842.

The cross is the guarantee of the gospel: therefore it
has been its standard.

—Henri Frédéric Amiel,
Journal Intime, April 15, 1870.

VI

THE MESSAGE OF THE CROSS

I

THE cross speaks silently but surely of God's *Love's con-* great love for sinners. For this reason it has *quering word.* become the sign under which Christianity has won its way in a world of sin. This is not a theory of theology. It is a fact of history. Wherever the religion of Christ has advanced, its song of victory has been the burden of the ancient Latin hymn:

> " Forward the royal banners fly,
>   The sacred cross shines out on high,
>   Where man's Creator stooped to die
>   In human flesh, to draw man nigh."[1]

The same burden is repeated in the latest music of the modern church:

> " Onward, Christian soldiers,
>   Marching as to war,
>   With the cross of Jesus
>   Going on before."[2]

[1] Venantius Fortunatus, *Vexilla Regis prodeunt*, sixth century.　　　　[2] Sabine Baring-Gould, 1865.

Nothing could appear more strange, if we leave out of view that interpretation of the death of Jesus which comes from the faith of the atonement, than that the cross, the emblem of the world's shame and reproach, should become the symbol of Christian faith, the treasure of Christian hope, the banner of Christian victory. How came it to be thus transformed? What miracle has exalted the instrument of death to the place of glory?

When Christianity came to China under this banner, the Chinese wondered at it, mocked at it, issued an edict against it. This edict said: "Why should the worshippers of Jesus reverence the instrument of His punishment, and consider it so to represent Him as not to venture to tread upon it? Would it be common sense, if the father or ancestor of a house had been killed by a shot from a gun, or by a wound from a sword, that his sons or grandsons should reverence the gun or the sword as their father or ancestor?" It is a searching question; and the only answer to it is in the inner life, where the cross of Jesus has been planted as the tree of peace and blessing, the sign of divine forgiveness and redeeming love; so that the first cry of faith is

"Simply to Thy cross I cling,"

and the last breath of prayer is

" Hold Thou Thy cross before my closing eyes."

There is a passage in the *Confessions of a* *The cross*
Beautiful Soul which tells the story of human *begets faith.*
experience before the cross.

" 'Now, Almighty God, grant me the gift of
faith !' This was the prayer that came out of
the deepest need of my heart. I leaned upon
the little table beside me, and hid my tear-
stained face in my hands. At last I was in the
state in which we must be, if God is to hear our
prayers, but in which we so seldom are.

" Yes, but who could ever express, even in the
dimmest way, the experience that came to me
then? A secret influence drew my soul away
to the cross, where Jesus once expired. It was
an inward leading, I cannot give it any other
name, like that which draws the heart to its
beloved one in absence, a spiritual approach
doubtless far truer and more real than a dream.
So my soul drew near to Him who became man
and died upon the cross, and in that moment I
knew what faith was.

" 'This is faith!' I cried, and sprang up as if
half frightened. I tried to make sure of my
experience, to verify my vision, and soon I was
convinced that my spirit had received a wholly
new power to uplift itself.

"In these feelings words forsake us. I could distinguish clearly between my experience and all fantasy. It was entirely free from fantasy. It was not a dream-picture. And yet it gave me the sense of reality in the object which it brought before me, just as imagination does when it recalls the features of a dear friend far away."[1]

Many are the souls that have passed through that indescribable experience. Millions of men who have been unmoved by philosophy and unconvinced by argument, have yielded to the mystic attractions of the cross of Jesus. The story of this divine charm runs like a thread of gold through all the many coloured literature of Christianity.

The cross in Christian literature.

If I were asked to name the three books outside of the New Testament which lie closest to the Christian heart, and are entitled to be called the classics of Christian faith, I should choose *The Imitation of Christ* and *The Pilgrim's Progress* and *The Christian Year*. There is no difference among them in their testimony to the power of the cross of Jesus to draw men to Him.

"Take up, therefore, thy cross," says Thomas à Kempis, "and follow Jesus, and thou shalt go

[1] *Wilhelm Meister's Lehrjahre*, Vol. II., p. 114.

into life everlasting. He went before bearing His cross, and died for thee on the cross, that thou mightest also bear thy cross and die on the cross with Him."

"So I saw in my dream," says John Bunyan, " that just as Christian came up with the Cross, his burden loosed from off his shoulders and fell from off his back, and began to tumble, and so continued to do, till it came to the mouth of the sepulchre, where it fell in, and I saw it no more. Then was Christian glad and lightsome, and said with a merry heart, He hath given me rest by His sorrow, and life by His death."

" Is it not strange," says John Keble in his poem on the Crucifixion, —

> " Is it not strange, the darkest hour
>   That ever dawned on sinful earth,
> Should touch the heart with softer power
>   For comfort than an angel's mirth?
> That to the cross the mourner's eye should turn,
> Sooner than where the stars of Christmas burn?
>
> *   *   *   *   *   *   *   *
>
> " Lord of my heart, by Thy last cry,
>   Let not Thy blood on earth be spent:
> Lo, at Thy feet I fainting lie,
>   Mine eyes upon Thy wounds are bent;
> Upon Thy streaming wounds my weary eyes
> Wait, like the parched earth on April skies.

" Wash me, and dry these bitter tears;
  Oh, let my heart no farther roam, —
 'Tis Thine by vows and hopes and fears,
  Long since.   Oh, call Thy wanderer home, —
 To that dear home, safe in Thy wounded side,
 Where only broken hearts their sin and shame may
   hide."

II

Doubtless the attractive, healing, convincing, *The blessing of the cross.* purifying, pacifying power of the cross comes from its silent proclamation of the holy and self-sacrificing love of God. It reveals Him to us as He really is, — eternally willing to forgive sin, and entirely ready to suffer for the sake of making its forgiveness perfect and pure and altogether beyond question. It carries in itself the marks of an immeasurable mercy; a tender resolution to meet, for our sake, requirements that are beyond our ken; a tranquil and complete assurance that God's pardon is a holy pardon, a righteous pardon, a pardon through which "there is no condemnation to those who are in Christ Jesus." [1]

But we do not say that this message of the *It comes to some who do not understand it.* cross is the only ministry of peace and blessing and enrichment that Christ has brought to the life of man. Nor do we say that those who have failed to hear in this message the very same words which it brings to us, or to interpret these words as they have been interpreted in our experience, have not been blessed in any way by Christ.

Some have followed Him, as Peter did at

[1] Rom. viii. 1.

first, unwilling to think of His cross. Some have trusted His forgiving power, as Mary Magdalen did, without apprehending what His forgiveness would cost. Some have called upon Him for salvation, as the penitent thief did, without understanding the great significance of His sacrifice. And there are some to-day who belong to Christ in their hearts and lives, but who have not yet read clearly the writing above the cross.

They are saved by Christ.

Pure and patient souls, companions of the merciful labours of Jesus, lovers of His gracious doctrine, worshippers of His divine perfection, illustrators of His meek and lowly spirit, whose lives are fragrant with the sweetness of the Master's name, of whose presence the world is glad, in whose lowly service the heart of the Lord rejoiceth, — surely of them we may say, *If any man have the spirit of Christ, he is one of His.*

The saving shadow of the cross falls upon these gentle lives, though they know it not. Unconsciously they are sheltered beside the rock that is higher than they. Christ did not die only for those who call Him "Lord." He died also for those who minister to Him without knowing it.

But the message which is proclaimed to the

world by these serene and untroubled lives, — *But the world of sin needs a deeper gospel.* it is certainly a gospel; but is it, indeed, *the* Gospel for which the great mass of men, sinful, struggling, weary, despondent, are longing? No; it is imperfect. It does not go down to the bottom of human experience. It does not meet the full need of those who labour and are heavy-laden under the weight of sin, of those who are tormented with remorse, of those who would give all that they have if they could blot out the fatal past and cast away the burden of their conscious guilt. Poor strugglers under the curse of evil, the vast majority of mankind long passionately for the blessedness of the man whose sins are forgiven, whose transgressions are covered. To such men the gospel of the Son of God, who bore our sins in His own body on the tree, is the real gospel, the veritable "glad tidings of great joy."

Christianity will cease to be the religion of the unshepherded multitude when it ceases to proclaim "redemption through Christ's blood, even the forgiveness of sins." Its true transmitters ever have been, and ever must be, those who consciously accept, believe, and trust the message of the cross.

III

The growing message of the cro . There is no final formula of the cross. Perhaps if it could have been put into a series of logical propositions, the divine sacrifice would not have been necessary. But God has seen fit to save men, not by a system of dialectics, but by an experience of grace.

This experience takes into itself all the permanent elements of the soul's life. It includes and interprets also all those elements which are progressive, the factors of man's moral being which are in process of development through the discipline of the individual and the race.

It has been well said that "one of the objects of the atonement is to form the conscience to which it makes its appeal."[1]

It would be strange, indeed, if, with the education of man's ethical nature, there were not also a real progress in the interpretation of the message of the cross. It does not change; it unfolds. It is not transmuted; it is translated.

St. Paul's experience. We can see how it grew in the epistles of St. Paul. It was the same gospel from the beginning to the end of his life. But it found new

[1] Alexander Mackennal, *The Atonement: a Symposium,* London, 1883, p. 19.

expressions and took larger forms. It meant one thing in Thessalonica, and more of the same thing in Galatia, and more of the same thing in Corinth, and more of the same thing in Rome, until, finally, it rose to its height in the epistles of the imprisonment, where it appears as the good news of the reconciliation of all things, "whether they be things in earth or things in heaven."[1]

There are three great ideas in which the human race has made an immense ethical advance. And it seems to me that all of these advancing ideas must have an influence upon our interpretation of the message of the cross, and must open new vistas of wondrous glory in the circle of its universal significance.

Three progressive ideas.

The first of these ideas is the unity and solidarity of mankind. It is characteristic of modern thought that, in its view,

Human brotherhood

"The individual withers, and the world is more and more."[2]

Vast sociological tables are compiled, covering the physical peculiarities and social customs, the arts and industries, the family ties and ethical conceptions, the forms of government

---

[1] Col. i. 20. [2] Tennyson, *Locksley Hall.*

and modes of worship of all sorts and conditions of men, in all quarters of the globe. The causes of the rise or decline of certain tribes are investigated ; the secret bonds which unite the generations on an upward or downward scale are traced ; the average intelligence of communities is measured ; the average welfare of the world is estimated ; the collective view of mankind predominates in the thoughtful mind of to-day. A stone is thrown into the water in America. Its ripples are followed and noted on the farthest shores of the islands of the sea. Men are many ; but humanity is one.

It would be singular and unfortunate if this new view of life did not bring new and larger meanings into the message of the cross. It must be the meeting-point of races, as well as the landmark of centuries. It must reconcile man with men, as well as men with God. It must be an opener of closed doors, a conciliator of estranged peoples.

The charter of the cross. The universal charter of the cross, — "Go ye therefore and disciple all nations,"[1] — forgotten and obscured in ages of particularism, revives in ages of human brotherhood. A gospel of limited atonement becomes a manifest absurdity of selfishness. Sacrifice for others — one man

[1] Matt. xxviii. 19.

for another, one race for another, and Christ for all — is seen to be built into the very structure of Christianity.

If the modern world is to hear the message of the cross, it must speak the language of to-day — the language of universal atonement and foreign missions.

Another idea in which there has been a great *The purpose* advance is the notion of law. In the first *of law.* stage of human progress, the concept of law is chiefly vindictive; it simply destroys the offender. In the next stage, it takes on a nobler aspect and becomes a system which inflicts retribution on the law-breaker in order that its majesty may be upheld and the peace of society secured by the wholesome restraints of fear. Under this conception, law punishes the offender in order that other men may be afraid to offend. In the third and highest stage, the reformative principle of law comes into clear view and takes the leadership. The regulative idea does not vanish. The idea of a positive guilt in crime is not lost. But both become subordinate to the higher idea of a moral purpose in law, — the rescue and reformation of the offender. Rectoral justice still remains a necessity of government, but reformative justice appears as the supreme necessity of a moral order of society.

No man can study the history of laws, no man can read the story of prison reform and compare the penal statutes of three centuries ago with those of to-day, without perceiving that there has been a wonderful progress in this direction. And side by side with it, not always with equal steps, but always in the same direction, we see a progress in the interpretation of atonement.

The larger scope of the cross. The old idea, that Christ died because God was insulted and must punish somebody, fades out. The conception of the death of Jesus as a mere exhibition of governmental severity for the sake of keeping order in the universe, becomes too narrow. The measuring of the precise amount of Christ's suffering, as a *quid pro quo* for an equal amount of penalty incurred by human sin, no longer satisfies the moral sense. The cross itself, with its simplicity, its generosity of sacrifice, its evident reforming and regenerating power upon the heart, — the cross itself leads the race upward and onward in the interpretation of its message.

Whatever else the sufferings of Jesus may mean, whatever unsearchable necessities of the divine government they may meet, they must meet this great requirement, this ultimate ideal of all moral law. Their end must be righteousness, their purpose must be "to make us good."

So the cross comes with a deeper message than mere vindication of law, or mere exemption from penalty. It says to every man: "Christ was crucified with thee, that thou mightest be crucified with Him. He died for thee, that thou shouldest not henceforth live unto thyself, but unto Him who died for thee and rose again. Rise with Him into the new life. Never despair. Never surrender to remorse or fear or death. Come up with Christ, come on with Christ, into the ransomed life." *The inspiration of the cross.*

There is one more idea in which there has been a real advance; and that is, the idea of sin. Here I do not think it is possible for us to trace the progress through the centuries, as we can trace the ideas of human solidarity and of law. But certainly there is in the deepest and best modern thought a more profound and vital conception of the nature of sin, than there was in the ages when it was imagined that a murderer or an adultress could "square the record" by building a church or endowing a monastery. I think we feel now, if we admit *The inwardness of sin.*

that there is such a thing as sin at all, that it cannot be in any sense a mere external. "The laws of God are written in the human soul, and the sin of man is a sin against the law of his own nature." [1]

There is an unnaturalness in sin which is the worst kind of unworthiness. It cannot possibly be taken away by any outward pardon, by any formal justification at the bar of a law which is external to us. Not only must the law which is above us be fulfilled, but also the law which is within us must be restored. This can only be done by the renewal of a vital communion with God, who is the author of both laws. He must be our deliverer outwardly and inwardly, —

> "Be of sin the double cure
> Save me from its guilt and power."

The cross and the Comforter. The cross speaks to us not only of the death of Christ for us, but of the life of the Spirit in us. This was the interpretation which Jesus Himself put upon it. He said, "It is expedient for you that I go away : for if I go not away the Comforter will not come unto you." [2] Certainly we have not entered into the full meaning of Christ's death until we have learned to

[1] Lyman Abbott, *The Evolution of Christianity.*
[2] John xvi. 7.

see in it the condition and the means of the dispensation of the Spirit.

I do not profess to know the significance of this on the divine side. Why the Comforter would not come unless Christ went away, we cannot tell. But on the human side the truth is not difficult to apprehend. The vision of Christ's suffering and death makes it infinitely easier for us to receive the Comforter. It breaks the bonds of that rigid and pedantic notion of God which exhibits Him as remote, inflexible, impassible. It shows us that He is great enough and good enough to suffer with us in order to deliver us from sin. It diffuses through the soul the fragrance of a new kind of forgiveness, — the only real forgiveness, — a forgiveness which not only blots out guilt, but opens the heart's door to the Spirit and restores divine fellowship.

Thus it seems to me that the message of the cross, because it is a living message, must be ever growing and drawing new words into its service, and charging them with richer meaning.

The unfolding of the message.

The theory of the atonement will never be completed until the discipline and education of humanity are completed.

I turn to the literature of Christianity, and **I**

find there the experience of peace with God,
through the atonement of Christ crucified,
uttered in a thousand ways, expressed in a
thousand forms which rise spontaneously out
of the varying characters and conditions of
men.   This is the strange thing, the beautiful
thing, the vital thing, about this experience.
It is not possible to reduce it to one fixed and
final statement.   It is forever changing, and
growing, and expanding, because it is a living
experience, an ethical reality, an element of the
moral life.   And as a man's thought of sin and
his knowledge of sin are deepened by living, as
his idea of God and his fellowship with God are
purified and uplifted by believing, so his sense
of reconciliation with God through Christ must
grow purer and deeper and loftier to keep its
place in his inner life.

*To each man
the cross
brings his
own bless-
ing.*

You come to a man with your theory of the
atonement, and he says, "Yes, perhaps it means
that to you, but it means something else, something far more precious, to me."   You come to
another man, and he says : "No doubt there is
truth in your view, but it is not all the truth.
Christ crucified means more than that to me."
And so it ought to be, so it must be, if the
atonement has a real place in the inner life.
We ought not to expect, we ought not to wish,

that it should ever be defined or explained in a formula valid for all men and for all time. Whatever it may be in itself, whatever it may be in its objective relations to God's government of the world, for us it must be a progressive, growing, expanding element of spiritual peace and power.

IV

This expanding message of the cross, then, is what I believe to be the true gospel for a world of sin. The heart of it never changes. "Herein is love, not that we loved God, but that he loved us, and sent his Son to be the propitiation for our sins."

Is such a gospel as this unsuited to the present age? Is such a gospel as this a low gospel, a narrow gospel, an immoral gospel, an obsolete gospel, a gospel to be ashamed of in the presence of learning and refinement and moral earnestness? Let the men whose hearts have been cleansed and ennobled by it — the men like Paul, and Augustine, and Francis of Assisi, and Martin Luther, and John Wesley — make answer.

Is such an experience as this an unreal experience, a fantastic thing, a thing of no great consequence, of no large influence in

> "The very world which is the world
> Of all of us, — the place where in the end
> We find our happiness, or not at all"?

Let the answer come from the triumph in the midst of sorrow, the courage in the face of death, and the steadfast devotion to every noble cause, of those who have learned to say, "The life that I now live in the flesh I live by the faith of the Son of God, who loved me and gave himself for me."

Is such a message as this to the inner life of man no longer needed, no longer of value, in these latter days of enlightenment, in these high places of culture? Let the unchanged, struggling, sinful heart of man make answer.

Burdened with the weight of responsibilities to which we have never lived up, disenchanted by the sad advance of a knowledge with which our vital wisdom has not kept pace, stained and dishonoured by sins of selfishness and pride and impurity and unbrotherliness and greed and avarice and anger, which our very privileges charge with a tenfold guilt, — delicate and self-complacent offenders, men who know but do not practise, heirs of all the ages, who have bartered our birthright, and declined our duty, and sinned against light a thousand times, — how stand we in the sight of God, in these latter days, without a Saviour from our sins?

Is this an easy age, a careless age, a peaceful, secure, sin-free age for the inner life? On every side, with growing knowledge, the shades of the prison-house close around us.

The moralists tell us of ever increasing

obligations, duties, demands of personal and social righteousness. Never has the meaning of sin as an offence against the brotherhood of man made itself so clear or so dreadful to the sensitive spirit as now. Never has the selfishness that pervades our social order, our political organization, and our commercial system been so fully unmasked to our reluctant and troubled conscience. We see our careless, comfortable indulgences dishonoured by the spirit of greed which rejoices in them without a thought of the misery of our fellowmen. We see our glittering luxuries stained with the blood of those who suffer and perish that we may live at ease.

It is not that this age is worse than those which have gone before it. On the contrary, it is a little better. But far greater than its advance in virtue has been the increase in its knowledge of its own vices and sins. The sense of human fellowship and mutual responsibility, the deepening faith that every one of us is in a true and vital bond "his brother's keeper," and the clearer recognition of our own share — passive or active — in the cruel influences that have bowed the back, and dulled the brain, and darkened the heart of "the Man with the Hoe,"

" And made him dead to rapture and despair,
   A thing that grieves not and that never hopes,
   Stolid and stunned, a brother to the ox," [1]

— these things have put a new and dreadful emphasis upon the exceeding sinfulness of sin.

It does not need that a man of to-day should wade through drunkenness or debauchery, should be guilty of theft or adultery, in order to find the bitterest experience of sin. If the Divine Spirit has touched him with this new conviction of a neglected, despised, dishonoured brotherhood, he sees again, as Christ taught His disciples, that the shame of sin lies not in the outward life, but in the inmost heart. He recognizes, in the delicate and dainty motions of his own selfish passions, a guilt which will seem to him deeper than that of the poor daughters of pleasure who walk the city streets. His own subtle ambitions, his intellectual pride, his self-indulgence, the complacency and arrogance of what he fondly calls his religious life, look him in the face with eyes as dark and threatening as those of the man who strikes his brother down in blind anger. Far above his self-flattered "life of comparative purity under the domination of conscience " rises the vision of the

[1] Edwin Markham, *The Man with the Hoe.*

true Christ-life of stainless sacrifice under the domination of love, — the only life that is acceptable in the sight of the All-Father God.

Yes, in the light of to-day, the standard of moral perfection rises, the requirements of a holy law of life appear more lofty, more searching, more exacting.   But while the standard rises, the inspiration, without the message of the Cross, sinks and fails.

Students of life tell us of the permanence and the power of evil, the taint of blood, the force of degeneration, the heavy fetters of heredity.   The God who demands so much of us appears more and more remote, inaccessible, unable or unwilling to help us.   What comfort can philosophy, with its vague and distant theories of God, bring to our hearts feebly fluttering in the toils of fate?   What consolation can art, with its cool and delicate visions of unrealized ideals, afford to those who are languishing and consuming in life's fierce, irremediable fever?   It is little, indeed, that they can do for us without a true gospel of salvation from sin.

We need, in this day of deepening insight, increasing labour, and heavier-pressing burden of the soul, — now, more than ever, we need to know a God who is not only above us, but also with us and for us. A God who is willing to suffer with His suffering children; a God who Himself freely pays the greatest price that ever can be paid for the vindication of the holy law of life and the redemption of mankind from evil; a God whose sacrifice is *the* Atonement, taking away the sin of the world, covering alike the transgressions of the ignorant and the degraded and the deeper offences of the enlightened and the privileged, and giving to all who repent a sure pledge of Divine forgiveness and help — to believe in such a God is peace and courage and a new hope for the world. Where shall the men of to-day find this Immanuel, this present, sympathizing, suffering, redeeming Love?

On the Cross of Calvary this God is revealed, crowned with thorns and enduring death for our sake.

> "The very God! think, Abib; dost thou think?
> So the All-great were the All-loving, too, —
> So through the thunder comes a human voice
> Saying, 'O heart I made, a heart beats here!
> Face my hands fashioned, see it in myself!
> Thou hast no power, nor mayest conceive of mine,
> But love I gave thee with myself to love,
> *And thou must love me who have died for thee!*'"

Printed in the United States of America.

The Gospel for an Age of Doubt.

BY THE REV.

HENRY VAN DYKE, D.D., LL.D.

A REVISED EDITION WITH A NEW PREFACE.

The Interior, Chicago.

" Dr. Van Dyke's ' Gospel for an Age of Doubt,' which is often called the finest apologetic of modern times, is constantly coming out in new editions. It is a book that ought to be in the hands — and heart — of every thoughtful Christian of the day."

The Academy, London.

" Dr. Van Dyke's lectures form one of the most eloquent defences of Christianity that we have yet met with."

The New York Times.

"The most vital, suggestive, helpful book we know in the whole range of theological writing at this period."

The Pall Mall Gazette, London.

" The book can be heartily recommended as a sincere and thoughtful attempt to show the consistency of Christianity with truth."

The Outlook, New York.

"In our judgment, Dr. Van Dyke's ' Gospel for an Age of Doubt' takes a high rank among modern contributions to the philosophy of religion."

Rev. Dr. Geo. P. Fisher, in The Expositor, New York.

" He has given us a fresh and instructive work which nobly justifies his triple distinction as a preacher, a theologian, and a man of letters."

THE MACMILLAN COMPANY, Publishers,

66 FIFTH AVENUE, NEW YORK.